Obtaining Long-Term Wealth in Real Estate

Sandy Ferrera

Obtaining Long-Term Wealth in Real Estate

Copyright © 2019 Sandy Ferrera
All rights reserved.

ISBN: 978-1-946203-59-5

Disclaimer

This publication is designed to provide accurate and authoritative information regarding the subject matter contained within. It should be understood that the author and publisher are not engaged in rendering legal, accounting or other financial service through this medium. The author and publisher shall not be liable for your misuse of this material and shall have neither liability nor responsibility to anyone with respect to any loss or damage caused, or alleged to be caused, directly or indirectly by the information contained in this book. The author and/or publisher do not guarantee that anyone following these strategies, suggestions, tips, ideas or techniques will become successful. If legal advice or other expert assistance is required, the services of a competent professional should be sought.

All rights reserved. No portion of this book may be reproduced mechanically, electronically, or by any other means, including photocopying, without written permission of the author. It is illegal to copy the book, post it to a website, or distribute it by any other means without permission from the author.

www.ExpertPress.net

Table of Contents

Endorsements 7

Introduction 9

Chapter 1.

The Benefits of Investing in Real Estate 13
    Low Entry Point 14
    Real Estate Offers Stability 14
    Someone Else Makes the Investment on Your Behalf 15
    The Art of Leveraging 19

Chapter 2.

The Basic Principles 23
    Never Get Emotionally Attached 23
    Don't Buy Today What You See Yourself in Tomorrow 24
    Don't Let Ugly Scare You 27
    Never Get Caught in Trends 27
    Look at Properties Based on Their Merit 29
    Don't Overleverage 29
    Never Buy What You Cannot Afford to Keep 30
    Don't Bite Off More Than You Can Chew 31
    If It Sounds Too Good to Be True — It Probably Is 34
    Know Your Market 34
    Appeal to the Masses 36
    Location, Location, Location 38

Chapter 3.

Understanding the Basics of Financing Real Estate 41
Local Community Banks 46
Where to Finance When You Have Outgrown the Bank 47
Equity Lines 49
Foreclosed Properties 50
Nontraditional Purchasing Options 51
1031 Exchanges 54

Chapter 4.

Finding Properties to Purchase 59
Hiring a Professional 59
Finding Properties on Your Own 60
Identifying the Right Properties 63

Chapter 5.

Analyzing the Investment Property 67
Location 67
Examining Price 69
Cash Flow 74
Multi-Family Units 79
Securing Financing 82

Chapter 6.

Protecting Yourself When Purchasing 85
Home Inspections 85
Research 86
Insurance 88
Partnerships 88

Chapter 7.

Understanding the Intricacies of Insurance 93
Mortgage Insurance 93
Basic Homeowners Insurance 96

Chapter 8.

Your ROI and Getting a Stronger Return 99
Finding the Right Professional 99
Finding a Quality Tenant 100
Getting Your Unit Rental Ready 100
Checklist 102

Pricing Your Unit 103
Marketing Your Property 104
Setting Up Showings 106
Avoiding Scams 106
Qualifying an Applicant 108
Accepting Payment 109
Managing the Relationship 112

Chapter 9.

Disasters That Could Have Been Avoided 117
The Importance of a Contract 117
Nickels and Dimes 119
Half a House 120
Liability and Litigation 121

Final Thoughts 125

Conclusion 127

About the Author 129

Glossary 131

References and Resources 137

Endorsements

Sandy Ferrera is a self-made businesswoman who has never kept the secrets of her success to herself. Since the day we met, she has always told it like it is without filter. This book is her latest triumph. By sharing the knowledge that launched her thriving national property management franchise, she shows readers the path to success — combining fundamentals that collectively provide a synergistic and fascinating study in real estate investing. Sandy allows readers from any experience level to place themselves in the context of their owner experiences and challenges. Each chapter is written in layman's terms and is replete with fascinating attention to detail that reflects the author's skill and experience.

COL® Scott Glascock MPM® RMP®
All County Colorado Springs Company

I've worked with Sandy Ferrera for 30 plus years, and her uncanny knack for real estate investing still astonishes me. She's a straight shooter with a solid conservative approach. Over the years, we've done hundreds of deals together, and I'm astounded how she hits a winner every time.

Tim Belscher
Real Estate Broker since 1982

Our family owns several hundred homes that are managed by Sandy's company. Over the past 25 years, not only has she maximized our ROI but also has added properties to our portfolio that outperform the average. She has a keen sense of what makes a good investment.

Peter Flachsmann

Introduction

At 53 years old, I'm married to a fantastic man, have four amazing children, and one adorable grandson. I am a self-made individual who started my journey as an entrepreneur at a young age. I didn't have a lot of money when I began, but over the last 30 plus years, I've been very successful in real estate. I have bought and sold hundreds of properties, made millions of dollars, and built a successful property management company.

In 2008, my husband and I franchised our company. Over the last 11 years, we have grown exponentially. We have a fantastic group of successful franchisees, and All County® Property Management has locations in over 15 states. My investment approach has always been conservative, and as a result, I have been able to weather the worst of economic times. I was not born with a silver spoon; everything I've achieved has been the result of hard work, dedication, and good decisions. I firmly believe (and have proven) that real estate is a solid strategy for building wealth.

It my husband's suggestion that I write this book. I was hesitant at first, but the more I wrote and relived my experiences, the more excited I became. I recognize that some of you may have dabbled in real estate and may not have had the best experience. I also realize that thousands of investors lost everything in the financial disaster of 2007. Regardless of your experiences, I am writing this book to help you achieve a positive outcome if you decide to invest in real estate.

I was one of those investors who bought a pre-construction condo in the boom of 2005. I had $60,000 into it, and in 2008, I had to get a loan for $280,000. At that point, the unit was worth approximately $175,000. To make matters worse, we had just franchised our business and leveraged everything we had. While this was a stressful time, we ultimately secured financing and found a great tenant for the unit. In the end, our real estate investments allowed us to weather the economic storm and grow our business as the economy continued to suffer.

Not all of our purchases have been homeruns. However, over the years, I have gained great insight and believe that real estate is an excellent opportunity to build wealth; I can confidently say that it may even be the easiest route to take, especially if you don't have a lot of money to invest in the beginning.

I want to advise you on how to avoid bad investments and share with you the strategies that have made us so successful. There are so many opportunities that small investors aren't taking advantage of today. Most people don't realize that more than one-third of all the housing in the United States is renter-occupied, which makes real estate an excellent opportunity to build wealth. This book will provide you with the tools you need to navigate through the different facets of real estate investing.

Not only will you be equipped with the knowledge to follow solid investment strategies, but you'll also be able to avoid costly mistakes. My process is not a "get-rich-quick" approach but an honest approach to investing in real estate and creating long-term wealth. It doesn't matter if you're investing in single-family homes, multi-family units, condominiums, or commercial properties. Regardless of the investment opportunity, this book explores the basic rules that I always follow.

Chapter 1.

The Benefits of Investing in Real Estate

Simply put, housing is a basic need. You might be surprised to find out that over one-third of all homes in the United States are renter occupied. Regardless of the economic climate, rental properties are always in demand, which makes for smart investing.

In the last decade, we have witnessed a change in attitude. Many segments of the population who were former homeowners are now looking to become long-term renters and avoid the hassles of homeownership. As a result, landlords can command higher prices and obtain long-standing tenants, recognizing a higher return on investment (ROI).

Land is a diminishing commodity. While the population continues to grow, so does longevity. Ultimately, we cannot create more land for housing. Therefore, the value of land continues to increase.

For investors, there are a variety of tax advantages that come into play, including depreciation, expense write-offs, and appreciation/future value that is not recaptured until the asset is sold. Real estate offers many advantages, and there are so many opportunities for the small investor. All it takes is one property to get the ball rolling.

The benefits of investing in real estate are numerous. For over 30 years, I have found it to be financially rewarding. Through the properties I've bought and sold, I've reaped the most significant gains from my long-term investments. Here's why you should consider investing in real estate:

Low Entry Point

> The entry level is minimum, but the payout is high!

One of the most significant advantages of real estate is that you can own a six-figure asset with a low initial investment. For an investment of $5,000, most people can purchase their first property worth $100,000. As the owner, you control the investment; you can exchange or liquidate the asset at any time without penalty from the IRS. Unlike a 401(k) or a retirement plan, real estate investments are flexible.

Real Estate Offers Stability

Today's investor has a variety of investment strategies at their disposal. Typically, higher-yield investments equate to increased risk, but real estate investments offer this kind of growth potential without the uncertainty associated with riskier products, such as stocks and bonds. Real estate provides a stable investment opportunity with good returns. For example, prices in the stock market change within minutes, while land and housing move at a much slower pace. Your potential growth is high, and you reduce the risk of jeopardizing your financial future.

After the difficult economic times of the late 2000s, many would-be investors became fearful about putting their money into real estate. While you may be hesitant, knowing and understanding the market is crucial. Most people who were in the business recognized that the market could not handle the rate of appreciation that was occurring. They also understood that the lending practices were entirely unrealistic. (I knew individuals that were borrowing 125% of their current property value. Under any circumstance, this practice doesn't make for a smart financial decision.) Sound buying strategies, coupled with a thorough knowledge of the marketplace, will result in strong investments.

> There is nothing in this world without risk. I want to ensure that you minimize risk while optimizing your return.

Someone Else Makes the Investment on Your Behalf

When you rent out your property, your tenants make the monthly investment for you by paying your mortgage via their rent payment every month.

Example: *You purchase with $10,000 down, taking out a mortgage of $90,000 amortized over 20 years at 7.5 % interest, with a monthly payment of $725.03 (principal and interest). The tenant pays $975 per month in rent. At the beginning of the first month —not taking into consideration any cash flow — the tenant is paying the interest payment, as well as a $162.53 per month toward the pay down of the debt. After five years, the tenant has paid a total of $11,788 off the balance of the loan on your behalf.*

Table showing pay down of the principle and interest over five years

	Interest	Principle	Ending Balance
Year 1	$6,681	$2,018	$87,981
Year 2	$6,525	$2,176	$85,806
Year 3	$6,536	$2,344	$83,461
Year 4	$6,174	$2,527	$80,935
Year 5	$5,978	$2,723	$78,212
Total Paid	**$31,894**	**$11,788**	

Also, while you own the asset, it increases each year in value (known as appreciation). The appreciation in our local area is slow and steady, as is the case for most markets. Typically, you can count on 3.5 to 5% appreciation in any given market. While this varies in different geographic regions, it is a conservative calculation for most areas of the country.

The following table illustrates how easy it is for your equity to grow. We examine the same investment outlined above using a 3.5% and 5% appreciation rate after deducting the amount owed for the loan.

Appreciation – Loan Balance Table on $100,000 Investment

	5 Years	10 Years	15 Years
Balance of loan	$78,212	$61,081	$36,184
3.5% Appreciated Value	$118,769	$141,060	$167,535
Total Equity at 3.5%	$40,557	$79,979	$131,351
5% Appreciated Value	$127,628	$162,899	$207,893
Total Equity at 5%	$49,416	$101,818	$171,709

As we see above, the longer you hold the asset, the more it increases in value. The home purchased for $100,000 appreciated between $67,535 and $107,893 over 15 years. Factor in your initial investment of $10,000, and you have more than tripled your money.

In the next scenario, let's look at the return on our initial investment at different time frames. Using the same $100,000 as an example, we'll calculate the return on the initial $10,000 down payment after appreciation and the pay down on the mortgage.

To determine:

ROI = Gain from Investment – Cost of Investment X 100

Cost of Investment

> To determine the annualized return, you must have a financial calculator; otherwise, various calculators will do it for you on the internet.

The geometric equation is as follows:

Annualized ROI = ((principle + gain)/principle)^(365/days) -1

Return on Investment

	5 Years	10 Years	15 Years
Equity at 3.5% less the initial investment of $10,000	$30,557	$69,979	$121,351
Compound annualized return–ROI	32.32%	23.11%	18.73%
Equity at 5% less the initial investment of $10,000	$39,416	$91,818	$161,709
Compound annualized return–ROI	37.65%	26.12%	20.87%

As lucrative as this is, it doesn't stop there. If you take the rent received for the property of $975 per month, less the mortgage payment of $725, *you* end up with a cash flow of $250 per month/$3,000 per year (before expenses). After 15 years, the balance of the mortgage would be $36,184.

> What other investment vehicle gives you the opportunity for someone else to invest on your behalf?

Another attractive benefit for investors is depreciation expense, which is calculated yearly based upon the value of the property at purchase minus the current estimated value of the land. For a residential property, depreciation can be calculated on a 27.5-year basis.

> **Example:** *You purchase a property for $100,000. The value of the land is $20,000, which makes the house worth $80,000 for depreciation purposes. Dividing $80,000 by 27.5 years allows you a tax write-off of $2,909.09 every year (against other passive income) when filing your income taxes.*

Along with all the advantages listed above (and unlike the constraints of other investments, such as a retirement plan), there are a variety of other tax benefits. Some of these tax benefits include expensing mortgage interest, repairs, real estate taxes, and any other costs in maintaining your rental unit. Travel costs can also be expensed if you travel a significant distance to check on your rental property.

The Art of Leveraging

Leveraging investment properties is an excellent strategy for obtaining wealth. However, you never want to over-leverage and find yourself in the position of not being able to liquidate the asset if necessary. Paying cash for property may appeal to you, but it is better to use someone else's money, and have it work for you. I will highlight this in the two examples below based upon the equations outlined earlier:

> **Example:** *You paid cash for a house valued at $100,000. If you rent it out, the tenant would pay $58,500 toward rent over five years at a rate of $975 per month. Assuming you invest the $58,500 in a conservative market fund at 2.5%, your interest income on the rent would equate to $4,213. After five years, with an appreciation rate of 3 ½%, your total would amount to $18,769. Factoring in your initial investment, in addition to your interest income of $4,213, your compounded annualized ROI would be 12.66%.*

Initial Investment = **$100,000**
Income (rent) = **$58,500**
Interest Income = **$4,213**
Appreciation = **$18,769** $181,482–$100,000 x100
Total Income = **$181, 482** $100,000
ROI = 81.48%
Annualized ROI = **12.66%**

If we use the same investment of $100,000, let's examine what would happen if you purchased 10 houses. The conditions are the same, except for the fact we use the rent payment to pay the mortgage. This example also does not include any cash flow.

Example:

Initial Investment = **$100,000**
Pay down of mortgages = **$11,788 x 10 + $117,880**
Appreciation = **$187,690**
Total Income = **$405,570** $405,570–$100,000x100
ROI = 305.57% $100,000
Annualized ROI = **32.32%**

While either scenario is good, you can see how leveraging can aid you in achieving your long-term wealth plans.

> Imagine if you could do the same exercise with 100 houses!

Chapter 1 in Review:

- Low entry point
- There is no way to create more land; real estate will always be a commodity
- Real estate offers stability
- You control the asset (unlike retirement or 401(k) plans)
- As you gain equity, you have an asset that you can leverage to increase your wealth
- When investing in real estate, you can use another person's money to grow your own
- The tax benefits are quite favorable
- Assets can be reorganized without penalty

Chapter 2.

The Basic Principles

Never Get Emotionally Attached

When it comes to any real estate deal, it's crucial **not to become** emotionally attached. Unlike other types of investments, real estate tends to tug at our heartstrings. When you are considering a potential property, you must view it on its merit and NOT how it appeals to you (which is easier said than done). Purchasing your first property will be very exciting, but no matter your end game, there's no room for emotion when it comes to making a business decision.

Investors often purchase properties that they have always dreamed of owning or living in. Remember that the property is an investment. It's not about you; it's about making money. Never lose **sight** of your priorities and always focus on your final goal. How do you want this property to perform? Anything you purchase should be with a target market in mind.

Do your research and keep your end goal in mind. When emotion creeps in, people lose money.

In my early days, I was at a real estate closing as a representative of the buyer, who started to get cold feet, and the seller was becoming very obnoxious. Because I was young, foolish, and hard-headed, I ended up buying the property on principle, an unwise decision based solely on ego and emotion as I was not in the position to handle the carrying costs — such as mortgage payments, taxes, insurance, and maintenance — nor did I have enough cash at the time to fix it up properly. While I ended up getting out from under it, I learned a valuable lesson.

Don't Buy Today What You See Yourself in Tomorrow

Never purchase an investment property based on what you think you want to retire in. People often believe that they should buy their dream house or retirement home and rent it out until they are ready to retire or relocate. In theory, this sounds great, but when you look at it from a practicality standpoint, there are many flaws. When you purchase a property with the intent to rent it out, your goal is to maximize your return on your investment. Though buying a high-end beach condo may seem attractive, it comes with higher taxes, insurance, and a monthly HOA fee. You will also experience a high turnover, which will increase your costs and require you to repaint and clean your unit after each tenant moves out.

Based on these facts, your ROI will be much lower. Realistically, ten years from now, the unit that you loved will be out of date and no longer fit your present needs. The better alternative would be to invest the same amount of money into several investment properties that will perform better. In 10 years, you could sell those properties and purchase the property of your dreams. Ultimately, it makes far more financial sense in the long term.

> **Example:** *You purchase a great condo on the beach for $595,000. It has all of the amenities that you want in your forever home, but it also comes with the high-dollar $750 per month homeowners association (HOA) fee. Because of its proximity to the water, you are also required to carry flood insurance, which costs $5,000 per year. Additionally, you must purchase wind and hurricane insurance for $8,500. Then you need to consider the taxes, which amount to $18,000 per year. Your investment has quickly become extremely costly.*

Before repayment of the loan, you have a total annual cost of $40,500, a monthly payment of $3,375 that doesn't include the mortgage. Once you add in the mortgage amount of $476,000 and subtract your down payment amount of $199,000, the amortized monthly payment is $2,628 per month for 30 years (in addition to the total monthly cost of the property at $3,375, which was listed earlier). In total, your monthly expenditure amounts to $6,003, and the rental amount on the property is $5,000. When you factor all of this together, you are left with -$1,003 every month (or -$12,036 annually), and that's not factoring in a higher vacancy rate due to the nature of the property.

Now, let's look at this same investment from a different perspective.

Example: *With an investment of $595,000, you purchase three single-family homes in a location that is further inland. You have no HOA fees, no flood insurance, and your hurricane and wind insurance costs $3,600 per house per year. Your taxes amount to $4,000 annually per house. The total annual cost is $7,600 per house ($22,800 for all three). Each home will rent for $1,995 per month, ($5,985 for all three homes). The mortgage amount is the same amount of $476,000 or $2,628 per month. Your total monthly costs are $4,528, including taxes and insurance. Your rental income after expenses is $1,457 monthly or $17,484 annually. Due to the nature of the property, it will always be in demand, and you won't deal with long periods of vacancy.*

Using the table below, let's compare these two investments:

Beach Condo vs. Three Investment Properties

	Beach Condo	Three Investment Properties
Acquisition Costs	$595,000	$595,000
Monthly: HOA, Flood Insurance, Taxes	$3,375	$1,900
Monthly Payment	$2,628	$2,628
Total Payment	$6,003	$4,528
Rent	$5,000	$5,985
Income/Loss	-$1,003	$1,457

> In this scenario, would you rather lose $1,000 monthly ($12,036/year) or gain $1457 monthly ($17,484/year)? Over 10 years, you're looking at a loss of $120,360 on the beach house or gain of $174,840 when you purchase the three homes!

Now you can see why it makes more sense to buy the three properties, sell them — and then buy your dream home?

Don't Let Ugly Scare You

If I were scared away from every ugly property I looked at, I would have purchased a whole lot less. To me, ugly is the smell of money. I'm not referring to half-burned houses or properties that are not structurally sound but a repulsive mess that someone has left behind. In my opinion, the nastier a property is, the better. Give me oozing refrigerators, smelly carpet, and psychedelic wallpaper. I will go in and transform it into a diamond that every renter will want. Never underestimate the power of a dumpster, some elbow grease, paint, and new flooring. Some of my best purchases were properties that others passed on. Keep an open mind; it's where you earn your sweat equity.

Never Get Caught in Trends

For most investors, trends can be extremely costly. Over the years, I've seen too many investors jump on the bandwagon of "up-and-coming" or "revitalized" neighborhoods. When you hear or see these words — run the other way! Let someone else take the risk. If no one wants to live in that property, it will be challenging to sell or rent out.

One of the new trends is tiny houses. I wouldn't advise anyone to purchase ten tiny homes. While this wave is popular right now, in ten years if everyone is upsizing, you'll be stuck with small homes that you cannot sell or rent. When it comes to investing in real estate, stick with Middle America or the average property. As different fads come and go, you want to make sure that your investments will stand the test of time.

> **Example:** *We managed several homes for one of our owners who was in the military. He was a delight to work with, and we had a professional relationship for roughly five years. When he called us to say that he had purchased four new properties from his friend who was in the real estate business, initially, we were very excited. Our feelings soon changed when he told us that the properties were in the newly revitalized district. My first reaction was to ask him if this was a done deal or if could he get out of the contracts. Unfortunately, he had already closed. Reluctantly, we started managing them for him, and from the onset, it was a challenge. Getting these homes rental ready was the easy part. Keeping them in that state was far more difficult because while they were sitting vacant, they were very attractive to thieves. (Copper is always a big draw, and in one house, not only did they take the copper, they took everything but the front windows and the front door!)*

They also stole the fixtures, appliances, windows, and doorknobs. As it turned out, they were unable to take the carpet the first time around, so they came back a second time! After several years of trying to keep these homes rented to quality tenants, we had to give our termination to the owner. They were just not cost-effective for us to manage. Not only did our owner end up losing those homes in foreclosure, but he also lost the stronger assets that were originally in his portfolio. Today, almost 15 years later, that neighborhood is still in the "revitalizing district," and we continue to refuse to manage properties in this location.

Look at Properties Based on Their Merit

When you look at an investment, analyze it with fresh eyes. View the property based upon how it will perform as an asset. Try to see it through the lens of your targeted tenant, thinking about their needs and lifestyle. For example, if you were 25 and had to rent a 2-bedroom, 1-bath duplex, would you want to live there? Better yet, would you let your mom live there? If you consider a neighborhood to be unsafe for your wife or daughter, you shouldn't invest in the area. While this is a loaded question, if you can answer it honestly, it will keep you from making a bad decision. An investment property should appeal to the masses for optimal performance. Anything located in marginal areas that may be older or unique in specific ways will ultimately cost you more, which will result in loss of rent or sales price.

Don't Overleverage

On the surface, this seems straightforward. However, when the economy crashed, so did the hopes, dreams, and bank accounts of many real estate investors who were overleveraged. Don't be wooed by financing that seems too good to be true. If there is an offer for 100% financing, it may mean that you will be unable to get rid of the property if necessary — a significant risk to take. I am a firm believer in having an exit strategy, which means having the ability to sell your asset. I've seen overleveraging put too many investors in bad positions. In the last economic downturn, many were either forced to sell their assets as short sales or lose them altogether. Don't make this costly mistake. Not only does it impact your long-term investment portfolio, it can also ruin your credit, making it difficult to purchase property in the future.

Never Buy What You Cannot Afford to Keep

Not buying what you can't afford to keep is similar to my advice on overleveraging. But here I'm focusing on a property that you want to flip. Television has made flipping homes look easy and lucrative, but the truth is, it can be extremely risky if you don't have enough capital or you cannot sell the home. A good rule of thumb when purchasing a home to flip is making sure that the property will be a good rental and that you can afford to keep it. If your answer to either of these is no, you should rethink your investment strategy.

> **Example:** *Recently, a house near our farm property went into foreclosure, and it was offered through the auction house. My husband and I looked at it, considering it a purchase opportunity, and decided to pass. There were too many repairs necessary, and after running the numbers multiple times, I realized that it just wouldn't work for us. Eventually, someone bought it. I wondered how they were going to make it work. After 120 days of renovations, they put the property up for sale. Six months later, when they still hadn't sold it, they put it up for rent. Ninety days later and after slashing the prices, the property still sits vacant.*

When it comes to investing in real estate, not only is it important to have an exit strategy, you also need to be realistic when it comes to pricing for sale or rent. I may be considered conservative in my approach, but at the end of the race, my bank account can determine who is really winning.

Don't Bite Off More Than You Can Chew

As a rule, never take on more than you can handle, especially as a new investor. It's important to do your research and take baby steps. While this may seem like common sense, a lot of investors get in over their heads. If you are buying your first property, avoid a big fixer-upper or an 18-unit garden apartment complex. Choose a property where you can gain some sweat equity with little fixes, such as painting, carpeting, and landscaping. A vacancy coupled with marketing time equals holding costs, and that can drain bank accounts very quickly.

Looking more closely at the previous example of the individuals that purchased the house near my farm, you can see how it adds up:

Example:

The purchase price = **$97,000**
The rehab costs = **$115,000**
Selling costs at 10% = **$25,000**
Mortgage payments for one year = **$12,000**
Utilities/lawn care = **$2,400**
Total invested = **$251,00**

Best-case scenario, the house is worth $250,00 (which they could not sell it for), and the last asking price was $215,000. Because this is a simple breakdown, consider that there are probably more monthly costs that I haven't factored in. What is even more concerning about this case is that they have not been able to rent it and are now are bleeding money. Passing on this investment was clearly the correct choice for us.

If you estimate that the repair costs are going to be $30,000, I recommend adding another 10% to 15% cushion. Use this same approach with your repair timeline. When pricing, you can always ask for more and lower the price if needed. However, if you underestimate the amount you need for repairs or holding costs, you cannot make those monies back. By adding a cushion, you are less at risk of getting in over your head. And never rely solely on home inspections. They are not always thorough, and there are important structural aspects that may go unnoticed.

Lastly, when you decide to invest in a property, don't get pressured into a deal. If something must happen immediately, I would caution you to step back and ask why. What's the worst thing that could happen? You could lose the deal, or you could lose money. Chances are, the result will not be in your favor. In that instance, I would rather find a better deal.

Example: *My husband and I made an offer on a property, and it was turned down. We were very disappointed because we felt it was a great deal. Six weeks later, the agent contacted us and informed us that the contract had fallen through. Because another buyer was interested, we had one day to make our decision. We arranged to walk through the house and garage apartment, which was tenant occupied. As we entered, we noticed it was very*

dark because the tenant had black curtains on all the windows, and the lights were low. After we went over our regular checklist, we decided to purchase the home. However, in our exuberance, we missed issues in the home and neglected to drive the neighborhood. As a result, we didn't see the food kitchen and the homeless shelter several doors down.

We acquired the property, gave the tenants notice, and started the rehab project. One day, we went to check on how the repairs were proceeding. As we opened the door, we saw the electrician jumping from truss to truss as they collapsed! He ultimately landed in a heap at my husband's feet. Luckily, the electrician wasn't hurt, but every truss in the roof system was gone — eaten through by termites. Buying this property ended up being a very costly mistake on our part. We made repairs and rented out the units, but the property was never a good buy. Fortunately, after a decade, we were able to sell the house and make a small profit, but as a rental, it never performed as well as our other investments.

> Never allow anyone to pressure you into making a deal. Take your time!

If It Sounds Too Good to Be True — It Probably Is

Remember the adage, "If it looks like a fish, smells like a fish, and tastes like a fish — it's probably a fish"? If a deal appears too good to be true, it likely is. Before you make a move and get into something that may not be right for you, ask yourself why a buyer is offering such favorable terms. In cases like these, it's always "buyer beware." Don't hesitate to ask a seller about their motivation. Honest people will give you an up-front answer; steer clear of those who don't. If a deal sounds too good to pass up, do your due diligence, and look objectively at the opportunity. Make sure you're not the one who gets stuck with a problem property the way we did.

Know Your Market

When you decide to invest in real estate, it's critically important to know and understand your market. It is not enough to rely on the opinion of professionals; you need to educate yourself on your market area before purchasing any properties. There are so many resources available to the public. You can use the tax rolls and the county appraiser's office to research the value of a property and determine what it and neighboring properties sold for in the past. The internet is also an excellent tool. Sites such as Zillow®, Realtor.com®, and Trulia allow you to explore current inventory and pricing. As you begin your research, remember that *current pricing does not equal value*. What is listed is the asking price, which may not be a true reflection of value. If there is too much inventory, generally the price is too high.

When determining how to price a rental, it always comes down to the rule of supply and demand. When I price a unit, I want it to be the most competitive, so I always price aggressively to get the unit rented quickly. It does not matter if mine is nicer than my competition; I want to be able to have the first-round draft pick of tenants and avoid the leftovers. By pricing my property a few dollars below everyone else's, I get it rented quicker. I also get a quality tenant who understands that they have received a good value.

> The longer you hold a property, the more money you lose.

Let's look at an example of how investors lose money when offering properties for rent:

> **Example:** *An investor has a rental that is nicer than everything else on the market and lists it for $1,995, which is higher than all the other rental units in the area. After 30 days, it doesn't rent, so they reduce the price to $1,895. Another four weeks go by, and they still aren't able to rent it. Now they try another price reduction, changing the listing to $1,795, and at this price, it rents immediately. But because the unit sat vacant for eight weeks, they lost $3590 in potential rental income (not taking into consideration costs for utilities, lawn care, advertising, and other expenses). Pricing the unit competitively from the start — even if they had to wait 30 days — would have allowed them to come out ahead. But since it took three months to rent, they lost money they cannot recoup.*

> **Example:** *11 months of rent at $1,795 = $19,745 vs. 9 months of rent at $1,995 = $17,955.*

> In this case, the investor would have made $1,790 more if the condo had rented earlier at the lower price.

In today's economy, properties that sit on the market for more than 30 days (for sale or rent) develop a stigma and automatically become less desirable. Keep in mind that rental prices are driven by supply and demand and

The Basic Principles

not what a property rented for in the past or what you think the rent should be. Therefore, you always want to put your best foot forward and market to capture a renter during that initial period. If you are not receiving enough interest within the first seven days, it indicates that your rental is overpriced or that there's some other issue with your property.

> Remember, current market conditions — not last year's pricing — dictate today's rental value

Appeal to the Masses

To make the most of your investment, you'll want to appeal to the largest audience. Today's savvy renters demand more than ever, so think about your target customer and what they might want:

- Avoid odd floor plans or one-of-a-kind properties
- Stick with a neutral color palette that will allow a prospective tenant or buyer to envision their furniture in the space
- Choose durable, attractive finishes and products that add appeal for customers and value for investors, such as granite countertops, commercial "wood-look" flooring, and ceramic tile
- Steer clear of trendy accents, such as feature walls, built-in furniture, or strong colors
- Don't cut corners when repairs or updates are needed. If you don't have the skills to make professional repairs, hire someone who does

- Consider staging — the practice of styling and furnishing a property — if you're selling your investment or renting a high-end unit or trying to move numerous vacancies in an apartment complex; it's an inexpensive way to showcase your property

Following these guidelines will assist you in finding long-term, quality tenants faster.

Which do you think would appeal to a potential renter: a 2-bedroom duplex in a college town or a single-family home on five acres in the country? If you guessed the duplex, you'd be correct. While the five-acre home might command more money, it appeals to a very particular renter, which means it could take several months to find the right individual or family to fill the vacancy. However, in a college town, housing is always in demand, so you won't have trouble renting the duplex when it becomes available again. Some owners are reluctant to rent to college students, saying that they're not as creditworthy as other potential tenants. My response always is, "but their parents are."

Location, Location, Location

Anyone who has bought or sold real estate has heard the phrase, "location, location, location" as the determining factor of a property's desirability. While it's true you can change paint colors, knock down walls, or reconfigure a space, it's not easy to move a house without significant expense and repairs. Therefore, it's essential to understand the area in which you are buying.

I recommend driving through the neighborhood at different times of day. Are people out walking or biking? Would you feel safe in the neighborhood at night? Research the crime statistics and look at the school ratings.

Know what surrounds your investment. Is there a railroad track nearby? If so, what times of day do the trains come through? Are you in an active airspace where planes might fly overhead? Are you close to a food kitchen? All of these outside factors will affect how quickly your investment property will rent.

These influences will also determine the price at which you can list your property for sale or rent. Typically, the sales price is offset by these contributing factors. Many times, you can get a great deal, but you need to be aware of these factors and how they affect your rate of return before moving forward.

> **Example:** *The house located near the homeless shelter and food kitchen that I mentioned earlier is a perfect example of the importance of location. Every time the house went vacant, vagrants would sleep on the back porch, which made it extremely challenging to get the property rented. Understandably, most potential renters were scared off when they saw homeless individuals loitering on the property. And the proximity of the food kitchen meant that we were constantly cleaning up Styrofoam containers from food served to the homeless (who decided to use our property as their dining area). But the worst experience had to be the fire that quickly engulfed the tree and fence but, thankfully, didn't burn the house down! Eventually, we put a six-foot privacy fence around the house — which ultimately backfired, as vagrants then slept on the front porch.*

If the property is a good bargain, the fact that it's close to the railroad tracks or within commercial airspace doesn't have to be deterrent. With everything else being equal, a 3-bedroom, 2-bath, 2-car garage home on a cul-de-sac and the same type of home near a railroad track won't command the same price. While they are still both desirable properties, you will need to adjust the rental price to compensate for the environmental factors and attract the right tenant. Conversely, when you're purchasing a home that is close to railroad tracks, you should be able to get a much lower price. And because more buyers are looking for a home near a cul-de-sac than one close to a railroad track for long-term owner occupancy, you may be able to negotiate more favorable terms.

Chapter 2 in Review:

- Don't allow yourself to get emotionally attached
- Buy what makes financial sense today — not what you see yourself residing in later in life
- Avoid trends, fads, and areas of redevelopment
- Every investment should stand up on its merit
- Leverage with sound financial decisions
- Purchase only property that you can afford to keep
- Be sensible; don't get in over your head
- Educate yourself about the market you are purchasing in
- Make sure your investment appeals to the widest audience
- Don't get caught up in deals that are "too good to be true"
- Location, location, location!

Chapter 3.

Understanding the Basics of Financing Real Estate

Once you've decided to invest in real estate, where do you begin? First, good credit is very helpful when you are growing your portfolio. Initially, you may have little or no credit when you purchase your first property. However, as you continue to increase your asset base, a strong credit rating will open more doors for you. Investors with low credit scores or slow pays will have difficulty obtaining funding, so paying your bills on time should be a priority.

The easiest place to start is often with your first home. Most first-time homebuyers purchase their starter home with very little cash down. Typically, the minimum required down payment for a conventional loan is 3% to 5% of the sales price. If you qualify for government-backed lending options, such as VA loans (guaranteed by the United States Department of Veterans Affairs) or FHA loans (insured by the United States Department of Veterans Affairs), or special programs for first-time homebuyers, your down payment could even be lower.

As you look to invest in your first home, there are a couple options to consider:

1. You can purchase a single-family home and, rather than sell it once you have outgrown it, turn it into your first rental property.
2. The other option is to purchase an owner-occupied, multi-dwelling unit. In this case, you would purchase a residential property with two to four units; you would live in one unit and rent out the others.

As you move on to purchase the next property, you will likely encounter another low-down-payment conventional loan option of 5% as long as you are planning on owner occupying the property. It too can be turned into a rental when you are ready to move up. At this stage, you are well on your way to becoming a wealthy real estate investor.

Example: *When my boys were young, we moved every couple of years. I would buy a home that was a good bargain and in desperate need of cosmetic repairs, and we would move in. I did most of the work myself with some help from my father. Once the renovations were complete, I would find another house to move to and rent out the one I had just finished, starting the process all over again. While moving so much was difficult on the children, I kept the boys in private school so that they could maintain their friends and offer more stability. We always made moving into a new home an adventure. I taught them valuable lessons about hard work and allowed them to see the possibilities in homes that most people would pass by or ignore.*

Using this strategy, I was able to grow my portfolio on a limited budget and build instant sweat equity. As I moved from house to house, I was able to expand my portfolio by leveraging the equity in these properties to purchase other investment property.

> **Example:** *I purchased one of my earlier properties for $50,000 with $3,000 down, taking out a mortgage of $47,000. After putting lots of sweat equity into it, the value increased to $75,000. After five years of renting it, the increased value after appreciation was $95,721. The balance of the mortgage after those five years at 6% with a 20-year amortization was $39,903.*

The new value of the house was now $95,721 (not including the balance of the mortgage at $39,903), and I had $55,818 in equity. So, I took out a second mortgage, or equity line, against the home for another $35,000 and purchased two more houses. In doing this, I still had over 20% of equity in the initial home.

As your portfolio grows, so do the lending requirements on future properties you wish to purchase. Long gone are the days of 100% financing or assumable, no-qualifying loans. The more properties you accumulate, the more money you'll be required to put down, specifically if you are using traditional financing methods. Most banks or regular lenders require investors to put down 20% to 30% of the purchase price.

One way to acquire property and avoid the hefty down payment is by purchasing property that needs work and paying for it with cash. After you make all of the necessary repairs, put a tenant in the home, and then go out and place the financing on the property; this will allow you to pull most of your cash out and give you a good basis for obtaining the mortgage.

The loan process will be much easier because you already own the home, and most lenders will loan anywhere from 70% to 80% of the improved market value on investment properties. I also try to maintain relationships with small, community banks. Typically, these banks offer portfolio lending, which I will discuss further on.

> **Example:** *I bought a 2-bedroom, 1-bath block home in Pinellas Park for $50,000. The value of the house would be $90,000 after renovations, so I put another $20,000 into updating the kitchen, bath, paint, carpet, and landscaping. Then I refinanced it for 70% of its new current value of $90,000 and took out a new loan of $63,000. Ultimately, this allowed me to purchase the home with only $7,000 out of pocket, including the costs to fix it up, which amounted to less than 10% of the current value.*

If you don't have enough cash on hand to make a cash purchase, another option is asking a relative for a short-term loan or taking out an equity line of credit on another one of your properties.

Different Types of Loans

When arranging for bank financing, there are different types of loans and/or mortgages with which investors should be familiar.

Adjustable-rate mortgages (ARMs) are often offered to investors and are considered to be a type of conventional loan. They can be beneficial because they typically offer more favorable terms on the first couple of years of ownership. Initial rates are lower for a fixed period, allowing investors to gain better cash flow early on. Once the fixed-rate period ends, an ARM's interest rate moves up and down with another interest rate called the index, which is set by market forces and published by a neutral party. There are several indexes, and the loan paperwork identifies which index a particular ARM follows.

Balloon mortgages are amortized over a set period of years (typically 30) but will become due and payable well before the amortized period. Here's how it works: The loan payment is based on a term of 30 years, but the entire loan balance is usually due within five to seven years. The repayment date will be established and detailed in the loan document. A balloon mortgage can be attractive when you are looking for future appreciation and plan on selling your asset before it balloons. If you don't sell the property before the balloon date, you will either be required to refinance the property or pay off the entire loan balance.

> **Example:** *An investor purchases a house for $100,000 with a loan of $90,00. Though it is amortized for 30 years, it is set to balloon in five years. While the low entry point might make this kind of loan seem attractive, in most cases, an investor will be unable to fulfill the responsibility of paying the amount in full and will have to go through traditional lending options when it comes time to refinance. The five-year appreciation would only amount to $11,876 at 3.5%.*

The closing costs for a new loan could be as much as $4,607 at 5%, which means that the investor would end up eating into almost half of their built-up equity. Also, this scenario doesn't factor in the current interest rates, which may be higher than when our investor initially procured the loan, so the monthly payments could be substantially higher and could significantly reduce cash flow. Before agreeing to these kinds of terms, make sure that you understand the potential ramifications.

If an investor is interested in purchasing a property with a balloon mortgage, I always recommend that the balloon be at least 10 years from purchase date. Normally, when it is amortized over 15 years or less, you can ensure adequate protection of the asset and your ability to refinance. Overall, I am not a huge proponent of balloon mortgages, especially when obtaining conventional financing. However, balloon mortgages can be helpful when an investor wants to utilize less conventional methods, but I will usually avoid them unless there are special circumstances.

Stated income loans are typically offered to investors based upon their credit score and self-reported income. They are attractive to self-employed individuals or to people who have difficulty providing proof of income. Investors often like this type of loan because they can close quickly with very little aggravation. But the downside comes in the form of higher interest rates and closing costs. Remember, everything has value. Even if the costs are a bit higher, this type of loan can work if the earning potential is there. Making some money is always better than making no money. Often, your real estate professional will recommend stated income lenders; otherwise, you can research them on the internet, but be careful to avoid up-front costs beyond credit reports and appraisal fees.

> If the terms are attractive, it can make sense to pay more.

Local Community Banks

As I've mentioned, I maintain good relationships with my local community banks. They are a good option for many investors because, while they still have qualifying criteria, it is not uncommon for them to offer more flexibility and a willingness to extend credit if you have a relationship with them. Even if you don't meet the typical lending guidelines, if they retain your loan in their house portfolio, they could modify their regular lending criteria and offer you the loan.

I always try to spread my wealth over numerous financial institutions, which allows me to increase my buying power. Yes, it is more cumbersome to have a dozen bank accounts, but the benefits outweigh the aggravation. If I purchase a property in another state, I always find the local community bank and set up accounts with them, which allows me to facilitate all my financial needs and open opportunities to secure future financing.

Where to Finance When You Have Outgrown the Bank

If a bank isn't offering more financing, where do you go? It doesn't automatically mean that you have to purchase properties with cash. One avenue that many investors like to use is the owner-financed property. It's a desirable option for investors because there are often no credit checks and only minimal down payments and closing costs. Additionally, the mortgage is usually not reported to the credit bureau.

However, finding these properties can be challenging. Though typically overpriced, owner-financed properties can still be a good option. I often advise investors not to get hung up on price; you can afford to pay a little more when you are getting more attractive terms and don't have to pay regular lender closing costs. If your closing costs are typically 3% to 5%, you can overpay for the property and still get a good bargain.

> Remember, private lenders that offer owner-financing rarely report to the credit bureau and typically don't check credit; closing costs are minimal, and the loan terms can be negotiated.

The following table illustrates this example:

Purchase Price	Closing Costs	Total Investment
$95,000	5% = $4,750	$99,750
$100,000	$500	$100,500

As you search for properties, look for ones that need repairs. In most cases, the owners are unwilling to make the repairs or don't have the cash to do so. If a property has been on the market and hasn't sold, often the owner is primed for an offer. Seek out properties that have been owner-occupied for decades and have no mortgage. Many retirees enjoy the benefits of owner-financing because it allows them the opportunity to get a safe and secure investment. Through owner-financing, they receive a much higher interest rate than they ever would have gotten from the bank. Rental properties offer another avenue to get attractive financing terms as the asset is already investor owned.

> Don't get hung up on price — terms can be more valuable!

Example: *I managed a home for one of my investors, and they decided they wanted to sell. It was a nice, well-maintained, 2-bedroom block home. While it had been an excellent rental, the owner was getting older and wanted to prepare his estate for his heirs. Price was extremely important to him, and he was asking more than he would have been able to get if he had listed the property. However, he was very favorable with his terms. Even better, the property was already rented and generated positive cash flow.*

I purchased the home with only $5,000 down and amortized it over 15 years with a 7.5% interest rate. The owner wanted $77,500 for the house, but on the open market, it would have only appraised at $72,000, which means I overpaid by $5,500. Since it was owner-financed, there weren't any loan discount points or significant closing costs. The monthly mortgage payment was $672.08, and the tenant was payment $850 per month in rent, so there was a small cash flow. When I exchanged it 10 years later, the home was worth $117,280, and I only owed $33,541 on the mortgage. Long forgotten was the money I overpaid as I reaped the benefits of my return.

Equity Lines

As I touched on earlier, equity lines and lines of credit are also reliable financing options. You can take an equity line against one of your properties that has significant equity. Typically, the lender won't want to loan you more than 80% of the appraised value of the home. However, this method allows you to leverage an existing asset to acquire another.

A line of credit, on the other hand, is an unsecured loan based solely on your creditworthiness. Though a line of credit typically carries higher interest rates and the terms are not as favorable, it can be helpful when you need more funds for down payments. With credit lines, the loan can be called due at any time. I enjoy using lines of credit, and if they happen to be called due, I always have a backup plan to pay them off.

> **Example:** *Many years ago, when the economy was doing well, I had an American Express line of credit for $50,000. When the recession of 2007 hit, the company canceled the loan and called all balances due, making them payable immediately. I maintained this line of credit for homes I purchased with cash and was in the process of renovating. Fortunately, my balance was manageable when the loan was called due, so I didn't experience any hardship making the payment. However, it could have been far worse if I had owed the entire line of credit and did not have the cash to pay it off.*

> Don't get in over your head–always have a backup plan!

Foreclosed Properties

Many investors like foreclosed or bank-owned properties because their financing terms are far looser than those of a traditional lender. The financing terms are more flexible for these types of properties because the bank holds the property in their non-performing portfolio, which counts against them for their FDIC-insured status. To get these properties off the books, they will allow investors to purchase property with more favorable terms than they would allow otherwise.

In cases like these, the down payment is typically well below the usual investor requirements. While these properties may offer a great investment opportunity, it is essential to understand that these homes may have been under foreclosure for many years. You will be able to see the obvious repair needs on the outside, but there may be internal issues, such as electrical, plumbing, trusses, etc., that aren't visible from the outside. Carefully examine a potential foreclosure investment before you purchase it. These properties are typically offered in an "as-is condition." There is no warranty or recourse against the lender should major problems exist. In cases like these, follow the "Buyer Beware" rule.

Nontraditional Purchasing Options

While some shy away from these types of opportunities, I have found that you can get a good buy if you get a little creative and offer wraparound mortgages. This method of purchasing allows a seller with very little equity in the property the opportunity to get out from underneath it. In this case, an investor gives the seller some cash and takes over their existing loan without getting the lender's approval.

Using this purchasing approach involves risk for all parties, but in most cases, banks will not call a loan due if the mortgage is paid on time, and the insurance is kept up to date.

Technically, the seller is still responsible for the mortgage. However, as the buyer, if the lender calls the loan due and payable, you must be able to obtain new financing.

These kinds of deals can be structured in a way that protects all parties, but those arrangements should only be made by someone with knowledge and experience in nontraditional purchasing strategies.

> **Example:** *I visited a couple who wanted me to manage their block construction, 1-bedroom home in a nice neighborhood. I suggested that they convert their family room into a second bedroom to be able to rent the property for enough to cover their mortgage. The house was worth $40,000, and they owed $36,000. If they hired a realtor and paid their closing costs, they would have to come to the closing table with cash. If they kept it as a rental, they would need to renovate and make it a 2-bedroom unit. Because they were moving out of state and neither option was feasible for them, I purchased the home using a wraparound mortgage. I paid them $4,000 down and assumed the monthly payments. The closing costs were minimal, and everyone walked away happy.*

Another form of creative purchasing is a contract for deed. Just as it sounds, this involves contracting for the deed, which means that you don't officially close on the property, and the title doesn't go into your name. A contract for deed can make sense for investors with adequate cash flow from renting, though it makes it trickier to take advantage of tax deductions. Ultimately, this method can be attractive if you obtain good appreciation in the property or when there is a good potential for cash flow.

A word of caution: Avoid putting too much money into a transaction like this because the asset is not fully secured, and there could be risks. When structuring a contract for deed, you should have a lot of faith and confidence in the seller.

If you are looking to secure or take over a property without closing or putting a large sum of cash down, you can consider a lease option, which is like a contract for deed except you are leasing the property with an option to purchase it in the future. The public is probably more familiar with the term "Rent to Own." Like the contract for deed, there also needs to be provisions in place to make it beneficial for the investor in the form of cash flow potential or obtaining adequate funds to secure future means of financing.

The largest issue with a lease option is the nature of the deal; it's just an option. It does not afford the buyer any real interest or protection in the property. I would suggest this method only in unique circumstance that allowed the investor to profit. It is important to note that both the contract for deed as well as the lease to purchase put the investor at risk if there are potential liens on a property.

Example: *For many years, we had managed a nice three-bedroom, 2-bath, 2-car garage home in a desirable neighborhood for one of our investors. His final tenant left the property, and it was time to do some sprucing up. However, he decided that he did not want to put any more money into the it. The house didn't need any major renovations — just paint, carpet, landscaping, and other minor updates to get it ready to rent again. He was divorced, and his situation was unique. While he owned the home, he was solely responsible for the property, and he received all the tax advantages. Our investor wasn't interested in selling because the terms of his divorce stated that once he sold the property, he would have to give half the proceeds to his ex-wife.*

With some creative conversations, we came up with a solution that benefited us both. I put together a lease option at $700 a month and assumed all responsibility for repairs to the home. This excluded major items, such as the roof, mechanical, etc. that exceeded $3500. He paid the taxes and insurance and claimed all the tax benefits. For me, the big benefit was in the form of cash flow. I moved into the property with my boys for about seven months and made all the repairs and updates, ultimately renting the house out for $1,250 a month, which provided me with a cash flow of $550 per month or $6,600 per year. I kept the home for another 6 ½ years as a rental until he finally decided to sell. In investor circles, a deal like this is also called a sandwich lease

$6,600 Annual income X 6.5 Years as a rental = $42,900 Total income before minor repairs.

> Before you agree to this kind of deal, make sure that you are aware of the other party's financial situation. Don't be afraid to ask for a copy of their recent credit report.

1031 Exchanges

Investors can use a 1031 exchange as a tool to reorganize their portfolio. While this is not a financing option, it offers an opportunity to buy more properties or divest yourself of an investment that is not performing well while deferring any tax consequences. An investor can sell a property, identify it as a 1031 exchange, and defer any capital gains. However, they must reinvest all of the monies (commonly referred to as the "boot") in a similar property or multiple properties.

Before you get too excited, a 1031 is not a mechanism to retrieve cash or avoid paying capital gains on a property that you have purchased to flip or have sold to a related party. It is simply a good way to sell a property and buy several properties or a larger property, such as a small apartment community.

There are numerous regulations regarding 1031 exchanges that investors should make themselves familiar with in order to qualify with the IRS. For example, you cannot personally take any proceeds from the sale and deposit them into your bank account. Some firms specialize in handling these transactions for a fee.

Before you begin the process, you should find someone who will handle the 1031 exchange for you. Timing is critical when executing an exchange, as you must identify another property or properties to purchase within a specific time frame. In my career, I have done many 1031 exchanges, and I believe that they are extremely beneficial to investors who wish to retain wealth and build a sizeable portfolio.

If you're considering a 1031 exchange, it's crucial to research your area beforehand. In a seller's market, it can be challenging to identify properties to purchase within the time constraints dictated by the 1031 guidelines. Depending on what you're buying, there are some cases where you can line up potential purchases before you sell yours.

Example: *I purchased a home for $65,000 and rented it out for many years. When the last tenant moved out, I did a $20,000 remodel of the interior. I realized that the new value of the home was $150,000, and I only owed $43,000. I sold the home as a 1031 exchange, purchased three houses using the cash taken from the sale as a down payment, and mortgaged the remaining amount. Upon closing, the new assets were worth $425,500, and I increased my cash flow by $6,000 monthly. Even without the increased cash flow, this was a smart financial move to increase my net worth.*

> **Which would you prefer?**

One house = $150,000 value vs. three houses = $425,000

$102,000 equity $102,000 equity

$1,200 annual cash flow $7,200 annual cash flow

Most people believe that there will always be better opportunities on the horizon and that tomorrow will always be better than today. From a conservative approach, I, too, would like to believe tomorrow will be better. However, I make every investment based on today's financial wellness, not what I hope will be tomorrow's prosperity. This theory has allowed me to weather any economic storm and consistently build wealth. I hope this strategy brings you success as well.

Chapter 3 in Review:

- ➲ **Pay your bills on time — good credit makes working with lenders easier**
- ➲ **Buy your first home with a government-backed mortgage for a lower entry point; purchase your second home conventionally with a low down payment**
- ➲ **Purchase a home that needs repairs and gain sweat equity by doing the work yourself**
- ➲ **Adjustable-rate mortgages offer attractive cash flow options for investors**
- ➲ **Stated income loans offer a quick financing method with little paperwork for investors**
- ➲ **Use community banks; most offer portfolio loans that give investors flexibility**

56 OBTAINING LONG-TERM WEALTH IN REAL ESTATE

- Equity lines taken against your personal residence or a home with substantial equity can provide you with the funds to purchase additional properties
- A line of credit is another way to access cash, but remember that these loans can be called due at any time
- Owner-financing is a great financing option when you have outgrown the bank
- Foreclosed homes or bank-owned properties offer investors more attractive terms, but exercise caution as these properties may need extensive repairs
- Creative options, like a contract for deed, wrap-around mortgages, and lease purchase are good alternatives to traditional financing but are for the more experienced investor
- 1031 exchanges are not a method of financing, but they can offer investors the opportunity to sell a property and acquire multiple properties without tax consequences

Chapter 4.

Finding Properties to Purchase

Finding properties to buy can be challenging, but if you're always looking, you'll find them. Remember, if it were easy, everybody would be doing it. If you have a real estate license or are a member of the Board of Realtors, you have access to thousands of properties, but it can also be quite pricey. However, there are many other ways to research and find properties.

Hiring a Professional

If you don't have a license, the first step is to hire a real estate professional who is constantly looking on your behalf. This individual must understand your target property as well as what makes good financial sense for you. Having a license doesn't necessarily mean that they understand what would make a profitable investment or a good rental property. As you make your first deals, your Realtor® will gain a better understanding of what you're looking for in a property. If you decide to use a property manager to manage your assets, they can also advise you and your chosen real estate professional on the current rental and market conditions as well as which properties will generate the strongest rate of return.

As you search for properties, ask your Realtor® to set up auto-notifications that will alert you as soon as something goes on the market. Your settings can also include price changes and other factors that meet your criteria. When you receive a notification, it is important to view the listing right away. Good deals go fast! If you a find a property that fits your criteria, don't wait. Don't be afraid to make offers. If you haven't received a "no," either you aren't asking enough, your offers are too high, or your terms were too good. While you don't want to be insulting, you have to focus on creating wealth for your future. I've said earlier, and I will say it repeatedly throughout this book — **do not get emotionally attached!**

> When sniffing out deals, you need to be "Johnny on the spot," as time is always of the essence. Move quickly once you're notified of a potential property. Remember, you're not the only one looking.

Finding Properties on Your Own

You don't need the help of a professional to search for potential listings on popular websites such as *Zillow.com*® and *Realtor.com*®. Just keep in mind that these websites are not always accurate, so you'll need to verify the information via the public tax rolls and the property appraiser. Other ways to access listings is through foreclosure websites such as *Hubzu.com*®, *Auction.com*®, or *Hudhomesusa*.

org®. You can also find properties through your local clerk of the court and many other avenues.

When using these auction sites, you'll typically bid on a property via the internet. In some cases, you can see the properties beforehand. Other properties are owner-occupied, so a drive-by will be your only viewing opportunity. While some auction sites require that a licensed professional make the bid, others permit bidding without a license or certification. There are a lot of great deals out there, but as the buyer, you must beware. Research is critical, as many of these homes may have defects such as mold, sinkholes, or even title flaws. Before you consider purchasing one of these properties, you need to do your homework to avoid potential disaster. If a home is owner-occupied, the process to have the residents removed is quite lengthy and can be very expensive. Become knowledgeable on your state's eviction laws before moving forward so that you are aware of what it is going to cost and how long it will take.

> **Example:** *We bought a house through an online auction. The home was an excellent deal, and we were excited about the purchase. Because the house was occupied, we didn't get to see the inside, but it was a newer construction block home, and we were confident that this property would be a "slam dunk." After we acquired the house, we knocked on the door; no one was home, so we left a note introducing ourselves. When the man called back, we offered him cash to move (also referred to as "cash for keys"). During the call, he explained to me that we would never get him out, something the bank had been trying to do for seven years.*

I still wasn't deterred, and we called our attorney the next morning to start the eviction process. We were floored when we found out it could take nine to 12 months to have the owner removed from the property; the excitement over our latest acquisition faded quickly. Luckily, we had a good working relationship with the law office, and they called the clerk of the court every day for an opening on the docket. After 4 ½ months, we finally gained control of the property. During this time, we had to mow the front lawn to avoid code violations. Fortunately, when he moved, the previous owner took out all of the cabinets, fixtures, and flooring — effectively saving us money in tear-out costs — although, I don't believe he thought he was doing us a favor.

Sometimes, banks will offer a group of properties for sale, a practice known as wholesaling. Obtaining a group of properties can be advantageous because it provides you with more buying power. However, there are drawbacks. You will not have the luxury of picking and choosing which properties you can purchase. Essentially, this is a "winner-take-all" mentality. Because of these terms, you may end up with properties that are in undesirable areas, require too much work, or don't fit within your portfolio. When considering purchasing this way, do extensive homework on the front end. Remember to factor in holding time, selling, and renovation costs. While this may seem easy with one home, if you are working with 25, the numbers add up very quickly and can eat into your profits.

> When purchasing foreclosed homes or wholesaling, the buyer should always beware!

Another form of wholesaling occurs when a buyer enters into a contract with the seller that gives the buyer a right to allow someone else to assume the contract. The main objective of this method is to allow the original purchaser to sell it to the next buyer for more money before they even close on the property. This kind of deal always makes me nervous about the margins.

Identifying the Right Properties

Properties that are usually ripe for the picking include units that have been on the market for extended periods or ones with expired listings. They're easily identified by how the number of days they have been on the market (or when the "For Sale" sign is taken down and no one moves in or out). When looking at these properties, you need to identify why they didn't sell or are performing poorly. Price is usually the most common factor associated with a property not selling. In other cases, it could be tenant occupied with a lease that doesn't end for an extended period or the result of deferred maintenance and repairs. No matter the reason, it could be an opportunity for you. When you are putting together a deal, understanding what you want to achieve with the property is extremely beneficial.

Example: *I once purchased a very nice 3-bedroom, 2 ½ bath home on a cul-de-sac in a great neighborhood. The owner inherited it and couldn't sell the home because it didn't have air-conditioning and only had a fireplace for heat. In Florida, air-conditioning is a must! It was in great condition, but everything was original, including the green, shag carpet. The owner couldn't afford to make the repairs to sell or rent the property, and there was not enough margin for investors to fix it up and flip it. I gave the owner $5,000 down, owner-financed, and put another $7,500 into it for central heat and air, carpet, and paint. Post-renovation, I was able to rent it out for $1,195 a month. By understanding the owners motivation and financial situation, I was able to structure a deal that was a win-win for both parties.*

Another way to find great buying opportunities is by knocking on doors or sending letters and postcards to run-down houses or properties that appear to be renter occupied. If you are unable to contact anyone at the home, you can get the owner's contact information from your tax rolls, which are available to the public and can be accessed through the local clerk's office. Remember, if you choose to approach a house, make sure that you are friendly and personable. Not everyone is welcoming, and it's important to be cautious when approaching a property.

Networking is also an excellent way to get the word out that you are in the market to buy. Join your local real estate investment club. Not only will you obtain valuable information about how they are acquiring properties and managing them, you will also gain access to deals they may not have been able to purchase or passed on. Additionally, advise your friends and family that you are investing. Tell them to inform you of any opportunities that they hear about. Some of the best deals can come from word of mouth.

Chapter 4 in Review:

- Always be looking!
- Hire a real estate professional, but make sure they understand what makes a profitable investment
- Ask your real estate professional to set up auto-notifications for new properties or price changes; good deals go fast!
- Don't be afraid to make offers
- Use websites such as Zillow.com® and Realtor.com® when not using a licensed professional
- Follow the foreclosure sites: Hubzu.com, Auction.com, Hudhomesusa.org, or your local clerk of courts, etc.
- Understand the methods of purchasing wholesale and decide if it is right for you
- Target properties that have been on the market for a long time
- Implement grassroots marketing: knocking on doors and sending letters/postcards
- Network, network, network!
- Join a real estate investment club
- Don't forget to tell your friends and family that you are looking for investment opportunities

Chapter 5.

Analyzing the Investment Property

Once you've found a potential property, you'll need to determine if making it part of your portfolio makes good financial sense. Always consider the following factors:

Location

One of the most critical factors to consider is location, as it will impact your investment in the long run. Make sure the property is in desirable area and that it will appreciate at a good rate. Typically, I steer clear of areas that are in redevelopment districts or high-crime areas. Though many successful investors specialize in low-income or government-backed neighborhoods, as a conservative investor and property manager, I have found that these units have never performed as well as my other properties.

Many buyers shy away from busier streets, but I've had great success with homes and apartments located on main roads. Not only do they offer great visibility for marketing, they are typically less expensive than a comparable home in the middle of a traditional subdivision, which equates to a stronger cash flow.

As you evaluate a property, keep in mind your target market consumer. Properties that back up to industrial buildings or those located near a firehouse or railroad tracks can be a deterrent to an owner-occupied. However, for tenants with less inventory to choose from or those on a fixed budget, these kinds of property could offer a solution that they might not have had otherwise.

To determine how a property on a busier street or in a less desirable area should perform in comparison: the rent should be equal or close to the comparable property with a slight adjustment on price for the lesser location. Essentially, you will have already benefited in the form of a lower purchase price, so your mortgage and monthly payment will be lower, a savings you'll be able to pass along to a potential tenant.

> **Example:** *We managed a 3-bedroom, 2-bath home that backed up to an active railroad track. If that were not awkward enough, the bedrooms were on the first floor, and the kitchen and living area on the second floor. The owner had gotten negative feedback from all of the other property managers he had interviewed, but I assured him it would be no problem to rent it out. After all, it was a 3/2 single-family home. First, I determined when the train ran, so that I could inform would-be renters. Then I priced the property below where a typical home of this type would rent and informed all of the potential prospects that I had done so, along with my reasons why. Not only did we successfully rent this home out for more than a decade, but there were only three tenant turnovers during that period.*

> A quality product with a less desirable outside influence can still make a solid investment for the long-term investor.

Examining Price

Price is a significant factor when you're deciding whether to invest in a property. If it's priced too high, it will not generate cash flow. On the other hand, if the property is priced ridiculously low, chances are, there will be some other issues that you will need to explore further. While most people believe that price speaks for itself, there's much more to it than that. When you factor price, you must also include acquisition costs, carrying and rehab expenses, insurance premiums, annual taxes, HOAs, and other necessary costs.

Example: *Property #1 is a 3-bedroom, 2-bath, 2-car garage single-family home is on the auction block for $90,000. The home has been vacant for quite some time and needs significant repairs. After having the home inspected and obtaining estimates, you believe that you can get the home rental ready within 120 days. The costs will be $62,000 (including carrying costs). The repairs include updating the electrical, HVAC, hot water heater, plumbing fixtures and trim, appliances, lighting, cabinets, flooring, roof, and exterior and interior paint — essentially, a complete remodel except for the plumbing and the walls. At the end of the 120 days, you will have put a total of $152,000 into the house. You decide to rent it for $1,900.*

In comparison, Property #2 is similar, a 3-bedroom, 2-bath, 2-car garage single-family home that is move-in ready. It was built in 2006 and has been well-maintained. The asking price is $145,000. You can rent it out within the next 30 days at a rental rate of $1,900.

Property #2 would net you another $5,700 that the property listed above would not garnish until after you completed the rehab — a difference between the two properties of $12,700.

If you are analyzing the properties just on price, at first glance, Property #1 is the better buy. Also, when you take into consideration that Property #2 is thirteen years old and will require future repairs, Property #1 may still be the more attractive deal.

Let's evaluate what we know: Property #1 is going to require time, resources, and energy to get to the finish line. You'll need to ask yourself if you are ready to take on the responsibility of getting the home ready. Property #2 is move-in ready, and you can walk into it immediately. Which one is more attractive?

The truth is, there is no correct answer. It all depends on your personal goals and what is going to work best with your portfolio, timing, and financial health.

Property #1 will have to be purchased with cash, and you'll have to pay cash for the repairs. After renovating, you'll have to put financing on the property. Overall, the price is still going to be lower, and the property will be in better condition, assuming you don't run into any unforeseen problems.

With property #2, you will be able to place the financing immediately, so you will only be responsible for making the down payment and closing costs out of pocket. Additionally, you'll be able to rent it out right away and take advantage of the cash flow.

Let's explore another lender- vs. owner- financing scenario with an overpriced property compared to a correctly priced property.

Example: *Property #1 is on the market for $110,000. Though it is only worth $100,000, the owner is willing to finance. His terms are $10,000 down, and he will finance the remainder for 15 years at 5.25% with payments of $804 per month. If you took the entire 15 years to pay the loan, you pay an additional $44,698 in interest. The only closing costs you'll have are the recording fees, documentary stamps on the mortgage, and title insurance. Together, these costs would amount to roughly $1,000.*

The total acquisition costs and interest for property #1 would be $155,698

Example: *Property #2 is correctly priced on the market for $100,000. There are no terms, so you will need to get a bank mortgage. You can put $20,000 down and obtain a loan for $80,000. In this case, your closing costs are going to be more because you will need to pay origination fees, discount points, appraisal, survey, lender's insurance policy, documentary stamps on the mortgage, intangible taxes, and some miscellaneous fees. These fees will add approximately $5,450 based upon two discount points and the origination fee. The loan is being offered to you at 7% over 20 years, with a payment of $620 per month. If you took the entire 20 years to pay the loan, the interest would amount to $68,867.*

> The total acquisition costs and interest for property #2 is $174,317.

At face value, the total costs of Property #1 are less by almost $20,000, but the payments for Property #1 are $184 higher. However, with Property #2, you have an additional 60 months of mortgage payments before the loan is paid off. You'll need to decide what is more important to you: cash flow or a quicker payoff. Personally, I always go for the faster pay down before cash flow. However, I am in a different position today than I was 30 years ago. If you had asked me that question back then, I would have chosen the property with the higher cash flow. Depending on your circumstances and needs, your priorities may change.

> **Example:** *We bought a 3-bedroom, 2-bath house on an acre of land in Monticello, Florida. It had been on the market for almost two years because it was only half renovated, and it wouldn't pass inspection for the first-time buyer. There also wasn't enough margin in the investment to flip the property. We negotiated a price of $65,000 and owner-financing over 7 ½ years at 5%. With $10,000 down, the monthly payments were $734. We put another $13,000 into the property for a new air-conditioning unit, remodeled both baths, and put in a new deck, new appliances, and made other minor repairs. Upon completion, we rented it out for $895 per month. We were happy with the cash flow, but we were even more excited about the fact the property would be paid off in just 7 ½ years. Imagine if you could do this 10 times? Before any appreciation or improvement costs, you would have $650,000 worth of assets and $107,400 in rent every month. If you dream even bigger and do this 100 times, it would equal $6,500,000 in assets and $1,074,000 yearly rent!*

The table below illustrates the previous example.

Number of Houses	Total Value	Monthly Rent	Annual Rent
1	$65,000	$895	$10,740
10	$650,000	$8,950	$107,400
100	$6,500,000	$89,500	1,074,000

> Dream big! If you had 100 houses paid off (each worth $100,000) with monthly rent of $1,000 each = $10,000,000 in assets and $1,200,000 in revenue!

You'll need to decide how you want to make your money work for you. My philosophy has always been to gain wealth as quickly as possible. Today, the faster that I can pay off a property, the happier I am. However, I also understand the benefits of using another person's money. I never want to pay cash unless I am going to put financing on a property after a remodel. There are times when I will sacrifice cash flow for a quick pay down. While a 20- or 30-year mortgage might get you started, I typically don't want anything for more than 15 years. (I also followed this principle when purchasing our homestead and other personal use properties.)

We purchased our current farm on a 15-year amortization and financed the 120 acres we purchased for our retirement for 10 years. If you do the math, your ability to grow your portfolio will happen faster if you can focus on shorter-term loans. I regularly caution investors to avoid getting in over their heads. Make sure that you are realistic about what you can afford in monthly payments. And always remember to factor in future vacancies, repairs, and improvements.

Cash Flow

This brings us to cash flow, which is a vital part of the acquisition of a rental property. Regardless of your financial goals, how much money the property will return is fundamental in building your portfolio. Like price, determining cash flow requires you to dig a little deeper. Cash flow encompasses more than just your mortgage payment and the tenant's rent. Essentially, it is your net after paying all your expenses.

As I mentioned when discussing price, cash flow includes taxes, insurance, HOA fees, carrying costs, repairs, and capital improvements. Simply put, cash flow is the leftover money you have after deducting any costs associated with your property. When I examine my cash flow, the one thing that I never incorporate are my tax benefits; I always keep them separate, as a bonus. I am only looking at the actual costs associated with the property against actual income. While the tax benefits are great, they don't mean anything if I can't afford the property.

Following is a comparison of two properties that are alike in size and structure, but that is where their similarities end. Though there is a difference in price and amenities, both properties would make desirable rentals.

> **Example:** *Property #1 is a 3-bedroom, 2 ½ bath, 1-car garage townhouse in a beautiful community listed for sale at $224,000. It was built in 1992 and offers 1,551 square feet. Located in a desirable area, the community offers amenities that include a gated entry and a community pool. The HOA fee is $210 per month. The community consists of 160 two- and three-bedroom units. Market rent for this unit is $2,495 per month.*

Property #2 is a three-bedroom, 2 ½ bath, 2-car garage stand-alone home priced at $239,000. It was built in 1999 and boasts 1535 square feet. Though it's not in a gated community, the overall neighborhood is nice. The home does not have a pool, but the back yard is fenced. The market rent for this unit is $2,375.

On the surface, they both appear the same, but let's take a closer look:

Property #1 (Townhouse)
Price = **$224,000**
20% down = **$44,800**
Mortgage = **$179,200**
Rent = **$2,495**
30 years at 7% payment = **$1,192**
HOA Fee = **$210**
Cash flow = $1,093 before taxes and insurance
Property #2 (Single-family home)
Price = **$239,000**
20% down = **$47,800**
Mortgage = **$191,200**
Rent = **$2,375**
30 years at 7%-payment = **$1,272**
Cash flow = $1,103 before taxes and insurance

Now that you see the details of both, which one makes more financial sense? To answer that question, you must examine a variety of factors. With the townhouse, you must consider the rental ability. While the amenities and gated community will command a higher price, there are other identical units to rent that will compete with your property, which could drive your price down and ultimately prolong vacancy.

Additionally, because the townhouse has an HOA, potential renters and buyers are likely to be subject to the approval of the association. Depending on **the schedule of those** meetings and the approval process, it could take anywhere from 14 to 45 days. This potential delay costs you money, and the association may ultimately deny your prospect. The approval process includes examining factors such as credit score, income, number of occupants, pets, total vehicles, and the number of units currently being rented.

Another consideration is whether the townhouse will appreciate or sell as quickly if need be. If there is a foreclosure in the community, how much will it affect your unit and drive your price down? It doesn't matter how nice your unit is; the neighboring properties will drive the price and serve as your competition.

On the other hand, the association will typically take care of the townhome's exterior. Unlike the single-family home, you won't have to provide lawn care or worry about external repairs. In comparison, the single-family home allows you to control how you spend your money, whereas the board of directors will determine the townhome's expenses. And HOA fees are subject to increases or special assessments.

So, which one is better? The reality is, both properties make for good investments. The final decision comes down to personal preference and long-term goals. An analysis of the pros and cons is essential before you make an offer on any investment property. Do your due diligence on the property <u>and</u> the homeowners association. Examine the HOA's budget. Do they have reserves? How frequently have they raised monthly fees or passed a special assessment in the past? Are they good to work with and easily accessible? How many foreclosures have they had in the last five years? What is the ratio of owner- and renter-occupied units? These added insights will guide you in making a good decision.

The insurance coverage is another important consideration. Typical insurance costs would be less on the townhouse, as the exterior buildings are normally covered as part of the monthly fees. However, this fee is usually a difference of less than $1,000 a year, providing you are not in a flood zone.

Let's take it another step further and say that the single-family home is in a flood zone, and the additional flood insurance is $3,600 per year. Also, the roof has reached its life expectancy and will need to be replaced in the next 12 to 24 months at a cost of $13,200. See the analysis below:

Property #2 (Single-family home)
Price = **$239,000**
20% down = **$47,800**
Mortgage = **$191,200**
Rent = **$2,375**
30 years at 7% payment = **$1,272**
Cash flow = $1,103 before taxes and insurance

Estimated cash flow = **$1,103**
New Flood Insurance Premium Per Month = **-$300**
Cash flow after insurance = $803
Cost of roof over the next 24 months/per month = **-$550**
New cash flow over the next 24 months = $253

Looking at the case study that includes the new expenses, the single-family home suddenly has a much lower cash flow. Before we continue, let's make sure we've considered all of the factors. Don't forget to examine the potential appreciation, the difference in annual real estate taxes, the ability to make your own decisions, and others. The following table illustrates the monthly expenses of each property.

Monthly Expenses

Property	Price	Down Payment	Rent	Mortgage	Insurance	Taxes	HOA Fee	Net
Townhouse	$224,000	$44,800	$2,495	$1,192	$65	$174	$210	$854
Single-family	$239,000	$47,800	$2,395	$1,272	$105	$180	$0	$838

This table shows that if you are only looking at cash flow, the townhouse is the better choice. From a personal standpoint, I would still lean toward the purchase of the single-family home. Even though the townhouse looks better on paper, I am always going to focus on the property that I have more control over. I also believe that appreciation will be better on the single-family home. While I would prefer the house, I am not against purchasing or owning properties that are part of an association; I've had success with these kinds of properties in the past. However, in this example, I would lean toward choosing the single-family home.

Multi-Family Units

Multi-family units can be intimidating to the first-time investor, but they're very similar to single-family homes; they just include more properties to consider. Before you decide to add a multi-family unit to your portfolio, there are some pros and cons you'll need to think about. First, realize that you are dealing with a much higher price tag than other property types. While this is a challenge most investors face, remember that you are obtaining a lot more units for your money.

Example: *You found a gorgeous, garden apartment complex. The price is $795,000 for 14 units. The makeup of these units includes six 1-bedroom, 1-bath units; six 2-bedroom, 1-bath units; and two 2-bedroom, 2-bath units, which breaks down to approximately $56,700 per unit. The down payment is $159,000, and the balance of the mortgage is $636,000. You obtain financing for 30 years at an adjustable rate of 5.25%, and your monthly payments are $4,286 principal and interest.*

To determine whether this investment will provide you with positive cash flow, you have to consider other factors that we have identified. While the expenses would still be the same, subtracting the HOA fee, you would have additional expenses including water, sewer, garbage, electricity for the common areas, lawn care, maintenance, a laundry facility, and other expenses associated with the building.

You must also consider the vacancy rate. A good rule of thumb is to estimate a vacancy rate of 10%. While most investors consider this estimate to be high, I believe it is better to err on the side of caution than to be disappointed in your return later. In analyzing expenses, you'll also need to look closely at the profit and loss schedule from the seller, often disclosed in the listing agreement. A sample profit and loss should resemble the following:

Sample Profit and Loss

	Monthly	Annually
Income:	**$9,450**	**$113,400**
Expenses		
Mortgage:	$3,512	$42,144
Taxes:	$916	$10,992
Insurance:	$250	$3,000
Water/sewer:	$1,200	$14,400
Trash:	$550	$6,600
Electricity:	$200	$2,400
Vacancy:	$945	$11,340
Total Expenses:	**$7,573**	$90,876
Net Income:	$ 1,877	$22,524

The data used for the sample profit and loss statement reflects the following numbers: 1-bedroom units rent for $600, and 2-bedroom units rent for $700. The 2-bedroom, 2-bath units rent for $825. Total monthly income amounts to $9,450. So far, it seems like a good investment, but we'll need to examine all the expenses closely. The return calculated doesn't reflect any maintenance and/or repairs or vacancy loss.

Now, let's compare this to the single-family home's return of $838 a month/$10,056 per year. Which one is better? Again, it all depends on your investment style.

To cover all the bases, let's illustrate a final review of the pros and cons between single-family and multi-family property types.

Single-Family Home

Single-Family Home	Pros	Cons
Strong future appreciation	X	
Easy resale	X	
Less turnover/vacancy rate	X	
Tax benefits	X	
Tougher to finance more than four		X
No income when vacant		X
Inability to live off one property		X

Multi-Family Property

Multi-Family Proper	Pros	Cons
Strong future appreciation	X	
Increased cash flow	X	
One vacancy won't break the bank	X	
Cities will often offer incentives	X	
Financing advantages	X	
Tax benefits	X	
More turnovers/vacancies		X
More up-front monies		X
Not as easy to sell		X

While both kinds of properties come with plusses and minuses, they both offer great appeal. For me, the deciding factor is always the overall deal. If I could buy the multi-family property at a great price, that's the one I would take. It if was market value, like in the earlier example, I would probably pass on that deal and purchase several single-family homes. Either way, you need to look at the financing aspects before you decide.

Securing Financing

As we discussed earlier, securing loans after you have accrued a certain number of properties can become challenging. You may be able to get financing on up to four single-family home properties, rented at $1995 equates to an annual income of $95,760. However, getting 10 bank loans for single-family homes would prove difficult, so you would need to look for other financing methods.

Banks are usually more comfortable lending for multi-family units since they are considered commercial or business loans. In most cases, lenders will require you to use a licensed professional property manager, and you will have to file an annual profit and loss report. Remember, financing is based on your credit and the property's performance. With single-family homes, the performance of the property is of minimal weight. All of these factors are also dependent on property location or the demand for housing in that particular area.

Another perk of investing in multi-family housing is that municipalities often offer incentives, which could include financial assistance that you could use to upgrade or repair the property's interior, parking lot, landscaping, exterior painting, and more.

To determine which investment will offer better potential, I cannot stress strongly enough that due diligence is <u>always</u> required. Investigate everything and hire a professional who understands the benefits of real estate. They can help guide you through the process, but, ultimately, follow your gut. Naturally, the first property you purchase will make you nervous, but as you continue to make investments, the easier it becomes. You will be able to evaluate which properties work best for you.

Chapter 5 in Review:

- Location, location, location!
- Know what you are purchasing and how it will affect your investment
- A quality product with outside influences can still make a solid investment
- Price is a significant factor when forecasting the benefits of an investment, but don't forget about acquisition costs, carrying costs, insurance, taxes, renovations, and other associated costs
- There is no right or wrong answer when analyzing stand-alone homes vs. homes in a homeowners association; understand the differences and how they affect your bottom line
- Leveraging vs. cash flow — know your objectives to determine the best investment choice
- Single-family homes vs. multi-family properties both have their advantages and disadvantages, and when purchased properly, both offer great avenues to obtain wealth

Chapter 6.

Protecting Yourself When Purchasing

Home Inspections

Now that you're ready to buy, what should you do next? The most critical issue is to ensure that you are protected.

First and foremost, if you are buying a property on the open market, make the contract contingent upon a home inspection performed by a licensed professional. Turn on all the utilities and go through every feature of the property. If problems are discovered during the inspection, you'll have an opportunity to renegotiate the deal or walk away. Investing $750 to $1,000 in a home inspection makes far more sense than potentially losing thousands. I would recommend that you include a termite inspection as well.

If you go through the property and you can't turn on utilities or perform the inspection, once it is under contract, do the inspection before you make the offer. Call your local utility companies to gather information. Ask them questions about the average electric bills. Find out if there are any outstanding bills or if the meter is still on the property. If you find out that the electric usage is above normal, there is probably an issue, which could relate to lack of insulation, inefficient heating or cooling systems, or much larger issues.

Also, call the water and trash divisions and ask similar questions. Determine if the property is on sewer or septic. If it is on a septic system, find out what the costs would be to hook up to city utilities and if there is a deadline to do so. You'll be better prepared to move forward once you know the answer to these questions.

In cases where you cannot gain access to the property, do as much investigating as you can from the outside. If you can safely peek through the windows, do so. Furthermore, factor in any unknowns and expect major repairs. Do not rely on the photographs provided to you from the bank or other listing sites. They may not show mold, holes in the ceilings, or more severe damage.

Research

It's crucial to find out everything you can about your potential new investment. Your additional research should include the following:

- Conduct a preliminary title search (in cases of absolute auctions or foreclosures)
- Do your best to verify all liens or encumbrances against the property
- Find out if any other party has claim to the unit
- Check your tax rolls on any back real estate taxes owed or for more general information

- Use county records to verify that there are no pending litigations or judgments against the property owners
- Visit your local building department to find out if previous owners pulled permits for improvements to the property, and determine if there are any outstanding or unpermitted items

If there are issues, it will be your responsibility to close them out, bring them to code, or tear them down. All of these actions may substantially affect your property value.

> **Example:** *I once managed a single-family home for an investor. He had owned the home for about a year before we took over. We placed a tenant in the unit, and during their tenancy, we needed to replace the air-conditioning system. The vendor pulled permits, and 10 days later, we received a code violation notice saying the room on the back of the house had not been permitted. After months of arguing in front of the city council, we were required to tear down the room. The costs associated with bringing it up to code were too high, and the owner could not justify spending the money. We lost the tenant, and it took three months to get the work done. In the end, it cost the owner thousands of dollars in repairs and even more in the overall value of the property. We eventually rented the unit again, but for less money. All the aggravation and lost money could have been avoided with a little up-front research.*

When examining a property, research the current deed restrictions. Additionally, find out of there is a homeowners association. If there is, make sure that you understand their guidelines about tenants. Some association guidelines limit the number of rentals in the community or how often a property owner can rent their unit. If the home isn't part of an HOA, it doesn't mean there aren't any restrictions on the property. Communities and municipalities may prevent you from parking commercial vehicles in the neighborhood or renting out the property, and some have set square footage guidelines. These conditions can affect your overall profitability.

Insurance

Before you commit, call your insurance agent and get a quote to insure the property. Verify that the home is not in a flood zone, which you can do at no cost. However, if you purchase a property and find out later that you must carry $3,000 worth of flood insurance annually, it will dramatically reduce your ROI.

> Stay away from flood zones. A $3,000 a year flood policy equates to $90,000 over 30 years, which is enough money to purchase another house!

Partnerships

If you don't have enough money to invest on your own, a partnership option allows investors to pool their money for more buying power. However, if you are purchasing with a partner, choose carefully, and make sure that you have the same goals and expectations. Don't leave anything to chance; have the hard conversations in the beginning. Discuss things like cash on hand, unexpected circumstances, rental pricing, and prolonged vacancies. It is also critical to determine who will be responsible for making the final decisions.

A partnership is a long-term relationship, so you must enter into one with a solid understanding. If you choose this route, I recommend drawing up a written partnership agreement beforehand, addressing any potential issues that may transpire, and always having an exit agreement. For example, include the following:

- Buyout and terms
- Expected income and expenses
- Ongoing capital improvements
- Final decisions
- The unexpected financial bind
- Tax benefits
- Liquidation

A good working relationship is paramount, and someone must be the lead. If the responsibility is 50/50 and you end up in a standoff, who makes the decision? Understand that even with the best-laid plans, circumstances change.

For example, I never want to liquidate an asset unless it is underperforming or if I can transform it into something more profitable. But when you're in a partnership and the other party wants to sell, you'll encounter a significant problem. Your financial situation may not allow you to buy your partner out. And, if they are unwilling to purchase something else, procuring a 1031 is extremely tricky. Therefore, if you have had a large increase in value and have taken advantage of the tax benefits, you could potentially face significant capital gains (something I always try to avoid).

If you discuss out these different scenarios before you get involved financially, they are much easier to manage when things come up. In my experience, because of my good working relationships, I could buy out my partner's share. I accomplished this by paying the initial investment along with a predetermined rate of appreciation with terms that were outlined before forming the partnership.

In another instance, I was in a partnership where we owned multiple properties together, and my partner wanted to sell off his share. We divided the assets by equal value and quit-claimed our ownership to each other, which allowed my partner to sell off his holdings while I retained the same value of property. My first choice would have been to keep everything, but since my partner was adamant about selling, it was the best solution for both parties.

I've said it before (and I'll say it again), NEVER get emotionally attached. If you find yourself saying words like feel, love, dream — RUN! The most useful advice I can give to any investor is to take the emotion out of any real estate deal; your focus should be on making money and building wealth. You can buy what you love later on in life. Right now, you must make decisions based on what makes the best investment. You need to find properties that fit your portfolio and are going to be profitable long term. Look at everything objectively and reap the rewards of your investment.

Chapter 6 in Review:

- Get a home inspection
- Check with the utility companies to determine if there are outstanding bills, liens, missing meters, etc.
- When purchasing foreclosures, conduct a preliminary title search and inspect as much as you can
- Investigate outstanding permits, code violations, or other issues that may be a problem in the future
- Research deed restrictions before purchasing a property supervised by a homeowners association
- Before you commit, get an insurance quote and verify that the property is not in a flood zone
- If you want to go in with a partner, set up the relationship from the get-go by outlining everything from the present to the future
- Never get emotionally attached!
- Buy what you dream about after you become wealthy – not now!

Chapter 7.

Understanding the Intricacies of Insurance

You know what to expect when it comes to purchasing a property, but now we must delve into a topic that no one ever wants to talk about — insurance. The truth is, nobody wants to think about insurance until they need it. While this may not be the most exciting chapter, it is vital to recognize how insurance can affect your ROI, as well as future value.

Mortgage Insurance

To start, let's examine mortgage insurance. Essentially, mortgage insurance protects the lender if you default on the loan and is available in a variety of forms depending on the kind of financing you are using. Conventional loans refer to it as private mortgage insurance (PMI), while FHA loans call it a mortgage insurance premium (MPI). Though VA loans do not charge an insurance fee, they do collect a funding fee.

Mortgage insurance is not optional but required by the lender — either in the form of up-front payments or through monthly payments that incorporated into your loan payment.

Lenders require private mortgage insurance on conventional loans with less than a 20% down payment. Typical costs of PMI vary anywhere between 0.2% to 1.5% of your loan amount on an annual basis. The actual amount will vary from lender to lender and is calculated based your down payment and credit score. Once you pay down 78% of your loan value, they are required by law to cancel your PMI policy. (However, once you have paid off 20%, you can contact the lender and opt out of the PMI. If you don't initiate the process, your lender may not do it for you.)

With FHA loans, the amount of mortgage premium insurance charged upon obtaining the loan is 1.75%, regardless of the loan to value ratio. For example, if you purchase a home and finance $285,000 through FHA, $4,987.50 will be added to your loan amount.

There is also an additional annual fee, but it is paid monthly through your mortgage payment. To calculate, first take the annual rate and multiply it by the average principal balance over the next 12 months. After you've gotten that number, subtract the up-front MIP and divide the annual premium by 12 to determine your annual fee. Unlike conventional loans, the amount will not be discounted, refunded, or removed when you have paid down 20% or more.

Example: *Your average loan balance is $285,000 and your rate is 0.008% divided by 12 = $190 per month*

$$\frac{\$285{,}000 \times .008}{12} = \$190 \text{ per month}$$

Figuring out FHA amounts can be rather confusing, but the FHA.com website allows you to access an application that will do the calculations for you when you plug in your specifics.

As I mentioned earlier, VA loans do not require mortgage insurance, but they do collect a funding fee. This amount varies based upon the type of veteran applying, how much of a down payment they are making, and whether it is their first time using the program (the amount can change if they have made previous purchases). Typically, these fees will range anywhere from 1.25% to 3.3% of the purchase price for the regular purchase of a home. Manufactured homes, refinances, and assumptions of mortgages are calculated at a different rate. In some instances, such as the case of a veteran who suffered a service-related disability, a borrower may not have to pay a funding fee at all.

Though these premiums add costs to your investment, being able to purchase a home with less than 20% down can be very appealing. Understanding how mortgage insurance works will help you determine your total acquisition costs as well as your ROI.

Basic Homeowners Insurance

Typically, homeowners insurance is based on the value of the loan. Almost all lenders will require you to carry it and name them as a co-insured (which is critical in the case of a catastrophic loss because their loan will be protected). In very few cases, the lender will allow you to reduce coverage and insurance based upon the cost to replace the structure. For investors, this is a more attractive way to protect their asset; the policy is less expensive because the land is not part of the costs to rebuild.

Basic property insurance covers losses for events such as fire, theft, and damage to another person's property. It also includes situations like fallen trees, injuries that occur on the property, and other circumstances. Read your policy carefully so you know what it excludes. Owners are often required to carry additional coverage for cases such as lightning strikes, hail, windstorms, and other natural disasters.

Investors buy a different kind of policy that covers their property if the types of losses listed above occur. However, those policies do not cover a tenant's personal property; tenants must purchase a renter's policy that would cover their personal belongings in the event of theft or loss.

If you don't carry a nonowner-occupied basic policy or if you have a limited liability entity or corporation set up that holds several properties, I recommend that you always carry a liability policy. This policy covers injury to your tenants and any of their guests. Even when investors choose to self-insure, I always recommend carrying a liability policy. They are very inexpensive and are worth every penny you spend if you ever have to make a claim.

Another critical fact that an investor should be aware of is that when the property is vacant, your insurer could deny you if you make a claim. To avoid this, you need to change your policy to a vacant property policy or obtain a vacant endorsement rider so that you are always covered between tenants. It will also ensure that you have coverage if you rent your property out on a seasonal basis. While the endorsement may cost you a little extra, it saves you the hassle of remembering to switch policies when the property goes vacant.

Additional policies exist, and investors need to understand the kind of coverage they need. Often, people mistakenly think that they have coverage — only to discover that they don't. When loss, theft, or other damage happens and they file their claim, they are often devastated when they realize that they don't have that specific coverage on their policy. These additional policies can include; earthquake, flood, hurricane, terrorism, loss of rent, sewer backups, mudslides, sinkholes, freezing pipes, and more. To prevent situations like these, sit down with your insurance agent to discuss the types of coverage that best suits your need and ask questions so that you understand what your policy excludes.

Chapter 7 in Review:

- **Understand the different types of mortgage insurance when purchasing with less than 20% down or using government-backed loans**
- **Basic homeowners insurance coverage includes covering the structure from loses such as theft, fire, and other types of damage**
- **Landlords must change their basic homeowners insurance to a nonowner-occupied policy**
- **Liability insurance takes care of injuries that occur on or about your property**
- **Vacant policy coverage is necessary when a dwelling is vacant for more than 30 days**

Understanding the Intricacies of Insurance

- Other natural disasters, such as flood, hurricanes, and mudslides, require a homeowner to carry additional insurance that is not part of the basic policy
- Sit down with your insurance agent to determine what type of coverage is required for your property

Chapter 8.

Your ROI and Getting a Stronger Return

We've discussed the different factors that impact the return you receive on your investment, but now it's time to take a closer look. Purchase price, acquisition costs, and insurance play a large factor. However, now that the property belongs to you, how can you increase your return?

Finding the Right Professional

I always recommend aligning yourself with an experienced professional who understands the rental market. Remember, just because someone holds a valid real estate license does not automatically mean that they are knowledgeable about how to maximize the return on your investment. While many real estate agents specialize in buying or selling, very few focus their efforts solely on property management. You want to find someone who understand the dynamics of the rental market.

Finding a Quality Tenant

Rentals, unlike the regular sales market, are driven by supply and demand. What was comparable 30, 60, or even 90 days ago may not be realistic today. There is a natural ebb and flow, and in some markets, price and vacancy are determined by season. The first step in increasing your ROI is to get the property rented as quickly as possible to a well-qualified tenant.

Unlike portrayals on television, most renters do not hire an agent to find them a house or apartment. If they did, someone would have to pay the agent for locating the property, which is usually the landlord's responsibility. Today's renters have higher expectations than they did 10 years ago. More and more professionals are choosing to rent instead of purchase; they want to get away from the hassles of homeownership and home maintenance and are looking for maintenance-free, stylish living. Features such as granite countertops and stainless-steel appliances didn't always matter. Now, they are a must-have for most tenants. If you put together a quality product at a competitive price, you will be poised to capture a long-term, quality tenant.

Getting Your Unit Rental Ready

Curb appeal is extremely important because it's the first thing a potential tenant will see. Even if you don't have a lush, green lawn, it is important to put your best foot forward and make sure that the outside of your property is appealing. Everything should be nicely trimmed. Add some mulch and flowers in the garden beds. The paint should be in good shape, free from fading or chipping. Trees should be trimmed away from the property so that a prospective tenant will drive by and want to see more. If the outside appears to need work, you'll to scare away good individuals.

Equally as important as curb appeal is the interior of the home. The walls should be freshly painted in a neutral color, and the carpet should be clean and in good repair. There should be no odors from pets or cigarettes. As you prepare the house, ensure that all of the appliances and cabinetry are clean and in working order. Additionally, make sure that the doors are functioning with properly working locks. View the property with an objective eye. Would you want to live there? Older properties are fine if they are in good condition, but, remember, most people don't want dated features. You will either need to price your unit lower or match the standards of the similar properties on the market.

Address any problems with your property, especially those that could be harmful, such as mold or mildew, before you put the property on the market. Mold is a big no-no in the industry, and it can cause landlords unwanted hassles. Avoid problems before they occur by ensuring that everything is in working order.

> A quality product will attract a quality tenant.

The following checklist will help you determine whether your unit is rental ready:

Checklist

Exterior

- ☐ Exterior paint looks good and isn't faded or peeling
- ☐ Bushes have been trimmed
- ☐ Yard has been mowed and is free of debris
- ☐ Planters have been mulched and look appealing
- ☐ All windows have screens
- ☐ Fences are in good condition
- ☐ A yard sign has been placed on the property (a great way to inform potential renters that your property is ready for them to call home)

Interior

- ☐ Everything has been freshly painted
- ☐ Baseboards have been painted and are free of dust
- ☐ Flooring is clean and in good condition
- ☐ Window coverings are in good condition
- ☐ Appliances are clean and operable
- ☐ Plumbing fixtures are in good working order
- ☐ Bathroom tiles are in good repair without cracks
- ☐ Windows operate normally
- ☐ All doorknobs function and locks are in good working order
- ☐ Garage or storage area has been swept clean
- ☐ Air filters have been changed recently

Pricing Your Unit

To optimize your return, you need to familiarize yourself with your competition and pricing so that you'll be competitive and can attract the largest pool of candidates. Being competitive often means pricing your unit a few dollars below your competition. If your competition has been on the market for more than 30 days, chances are, they are overpriced. And if you use their numbers, you will be overpriced too. Remember, the more days your property sits vacant, the more money you lose.

Many investors believe that if they put a high price on their unit, they will attract a better-quality tenant. In reality, it's quite the opposite. Undesirable tenants are usually willing to take overpriced properties that need repair because they know that the quality properties will not accept them. Think of this, if you were recruiting for a sports team, would you want the first pick, or the last person left? It's no different for us. As an investor, you want to build wealth, and quality tenants will help you achieve your goals. A tenant who doesn't pay their bills on time is going to cost you money. Additionally, overpriced properties that sit on the market for more than 30 days ultimately develop a stigma.

> A home worth $2000 per month that sits vacant for 45 days equals a loss of $3000

Days vacant = a loss you never recoup

Marketing Your Property

Once your property is rental ready, the next step is marketing the unit to prospective tenants. In today's digital age, renters use a computer or cellphone to locate their next home. Craigslist is ancient history; today, people are utilizing sites like *Zillow.com*®, *Realtor.com*®, *Zumper.com*, and others. These websites provide access to far more information than tenants ever had before. Users can look at photographs, take virtual tours, find out how long the property has been on the market, and examine suggested rental prices. They can also analyze current market trends and compare properties.

The first rule of marketing is reaching your target audience. Start with the internet because it has the most reach. Most property management professionals subscribe to the services above. Additionally, they will usually market their listings on dozens (if not hundreds) of different sites. Since there is typically a cost associated with these services, you will need to analyze your market and determine which sites rank the highest and are the most used in your area so that you can prioritize. Typically, the ads run for 30+ days and allow you to add photos, virtual tours, and other details about your property. There are also some sites, such as Realtor.com®, that require the assistance of a licensed professional before posting a listing.

When you post your property for rent, you'll want to use quality photos and videos that showcase the property's features in a positive light. Avoid adding information that might be viewed as negative; if the property only has one bathroom, don't highlight that feature but, instead, focus on its more desirable and attractive amenities. You don't want potential tenants to click past your listing. Hire a professional if you can't take quality pictures or videos on your own. Write engaging and interesting ad copy that will entice a potential renter to view your listing. If you don't add quality photos or a solid write-up, potential customers will pass over your listing and go in search of something better.

> A picture is worth a thousand words; make sure your posts appeal to a broad population base.

Yard signs are also an excellent way to attract potential renters who want to rent in your neighborhood. Add a flyer that gives them details, pricing information, and ways to contact you. If the home is vacant, regularly check on the house to make sure that the property is secured, and everything looks good.

Another avenue to market your property is through social media. Some platforms allow you to post photos and descriptions of your property. Local newspapers and magazines can also help get the word out. However, these can sometimes be costly and slower to attract renters' attention. If you are in a community that offers bulletin boards, it's good practice to post your flyer there too.

Investors who own four or more units are required by law to follow all Fair Housing laws. These laws include restrictions on advertising. If you fall into this category, familiarize yourself with the requirements so that you comply with the regulations. Some words to avoid include exclusionary terms, such as "no children," "singles-only," "mature individuals," etc. Suggested guidelines can be found through the National Association of Realtors® or HUD (U.S. Department of Housing and Urban Development). The Americans with Disabilities Act of 1990 prohibits discrimination against individuals with disabilities. As an investor/property owner, you must be aware of and understand these laws.

Setting Up Showings

Before you set up a meeting with potential tenants, you'll want to get some preliminary information from them. In addition to getting their contact details, find out what they are looking for in a rental as you might have another property that is even better suited to their needs.

Try to restrict showings to daylight hours and, as a safety precaution, let potential tenants self-show the unit and move around freely while you remain outside. After they have toured the property, you can answer any questions that they may have and lock up.

Set up cattle calls to allow for multiple viewings at a time, or hold an open house, indicating the date and hours on your sign and in your ad. When sitting at an open house, I always recommend that you have someone with you, so you're not alone and have someone to help if multiple prospective tenants show up at once.

Avoiding Scams

When marketing your property, you'll need to be aware of potential scams. Unfortunately, there are many scammers out there who will steal your ads, change your locks, and rent the property before you even know it. Others target vacant properties and move into them because they know it will be difficult for the landlord to have them removed.

Be cautious as you market your property, and always place identifying materials in the unit that list you as the landlord.

We display signage in the interior of all our properties that lists our property management company along with our logo and contact numbers. Our company also watermarks any photos, videos, or marketing and advertising materials with our logo and company name.

One of the best ways to evade these problems is by avoiding sites that are known to attract scammers. Unprofessional websites can hijack your listing and rent your property out from under you. If this happens, you may end up getting stuck with a tenant you know nothing about. What makes this situation even more frustrating is that you will have to spend time and money evicting the person from your property, which can be very expensive. Depending on the state you live in, it can take quite a lot of energy and resources to get rid of them. Unfortunately, in most states, you cannot just call the police and have them removed but, instead, must go through a formal eviction.

> Be safe and smart when marketing your property to the general public.

Example: *Many years ago, we picked up a new rental property that belonged to an investor who had been trying to rent it on his own. We advised him that the property needed to be cleaned and the trash hauled away before we could start actively marketing the property, as the previous tenant had left furniture and belongings in the unit.*

Our investor signed the management agreement, gave us the keys, and allowed us to order the work. We removed his sign and had him take down any active ads. The next day, our handyman went to the house and removed two loads of leftover belongings from the property, but because it was getting dark, he planned to return the following day to finish the job.

But when he showed up the next day, the keys for the front lock didn't work. After trying several doors, he found that the garage was open and went in. Immediately, he noticed *that there appeared to be more belongings in the house than there had been the day before, but he started loading up his truck and didn't give it another thought. About an hour later, a woman showed and asked him why he was removing her possessions from the house she had just rented. Our handyman called us, and then we contacted local law enforcement. In this case, the woman had rented the home from someone other than our investor. Fortunately, she did not have a lease or proof that she had paid this person, so we were able to get the home back without having to go through a costly eviction. In this case, we were extremely lucky, but it doesn't usually work out that way.*

Qualifying an Applicant

Once someone is interested in your property, have them fill out an application. Regardless of how well your prospective tenants present themselves, you should screen every potential occupant 18 years or older to make sure they don't have a criminal record. I'll also caution you against "judging a book by its cover." Twenty-five years ago, if someone dressed nicely and drove a newer model vehicle, you assumed they had good credit. This assumption no longer applies. Never skip a background check before turning the keys over.

You'll want to run a credit check on your potential tenant to find out how they pay their bills. If they're not making their car payment on time, chances are, they won't pay you on time either. There are fee-based services that will run credit checks for landlords. As you do this, keep in mind the Fair Credit Reporting Act, which was enacted to protect consumers and regulate the collection of their credit information and access to their credit reports.

In some cases, the credit reporting company will do a criminal and civil background check, but if they don't, you can search public courthouse records in person or online to identify criminal acts, prior evictions, bankruptcies, or judgments. Also, check public websites to verify that your potential tenant isn't a sexual predator.

Be cautious when you are vetting potential tenants. For more background information, get a rental verification from their current and past landlords. If they are not renting from an apartment community or a professional real estate management company, make sure that the landlord's name matches the owner of record from your public records search. Potential renters who have had issues with previous landlords will often give false information so they you receive a glowing review.

Accepting Payment

Never accept someone with an elaborate "sob" story who needs to move in right away with a wad of cash. Good tenants do not wait until the last minute to find rentals. If someone has been displaced by fire, an act of God, or some other extraordinary situation, you'll be able to verify their story; don't take their word for it. Also, never accept move-in monies in the form of a personal check because if it bounces it could take you months to get your renter out, and you may not recoup the money.

> **Example:** *We inherited the management of an upscale, 3-bedroom, 2-bath, executive home with a garage in a great neighborhood from an owner who had originally hired another property management company. The prospective tenant, a well-dressed, extremely attractive woman with an adorable little girl, met with the management company's representative after hours on a Friday. The woman drove a late-model Mercedes and likely seemed to*

be the perfect tenant. The agent accepted the application fee, the first month's rent, and the security deposit in the form of a personal check. He also gave authorization for her to install new landscaping and sprinklers.

On Monday morning, the agent deposited the check. He hadn't processed a credit or background check on this tenant, and at the end of the week, the bank notified the agent that the check had been returned. He tried to reach the tenant, but he couldn't, so he drove to the property. The tenant wasn't there, but the landscaping was complete.

Since he couldn't reach her, he left her a note. Later in the week, he heard from the landscaping company informing him that the $4,000 check she wrote to them had bounced too. Three months later and without ever receiving a penny, he got the house back. It wasn't a case of eviction; the woman had been extradited to another state to stand trial for murdering her husband and for insurance fraud!

When you accept a tenant, always collect an adequate security deposit. The security deposit ensures the faithful performance of the lease and will cover any damage the tenant may cause during their tenancy. Common practice is to charge enough to cover at least one month's rent. In some cases, the landlord may also choose to charge for the last month's rent as well. Make sure that you are aware of your state's rental laws, as restrictions on the security deposit and last month's rent vary in different parts of the country.

Never take a deposit in the form of a personal check, IOU, or in exchange for work on the property. More landlords get burned when they allow these types of alternative forms of payment. Checks bounce, IOU's aren't' fulfilled, and the work for pay doesn't get done or is below standard. You don't want to get stuck trying to collect your payment. All move-in monies should be in the form of a cashier's check or a money order.

Remember, when you are trying to get a quality tenant who is going to pay and stay, never barter; the landlord always loses. You want to develop a long-term, successful relationship, and a quality product will attract a quality applicant. If a tenant is already trying to negotiate and wiggle out of terms in the beginning, imagine what could happen three months down the road.

Example: *I received a call from a potential owner who had rented her home to a very nice couple. The renters had taken the home "as is." The rent was at $1,250 per month, but they made an arrangement: In exchange for not having to pay the first month's rent or a security deposit, the tenants agreed that they would paint, clean up the yard, and make some minor repairs. The owner was desperate because she had been trying to rent the property out for two months with no success. Three months later, the landlord hadn't received any rent, and the tenant hadn't made any of the repairs. They hadn't even mowed the lawn, so the landlord was now receiving notifications from the city. She hired us, and we evicted the tenants, but the owner lost five months of rent and was left with even more repairs than before. The entire situation could have been avoided if she had gotten the property rental ready in the first place. Unfortunately, this is not a unique story; I have helped hundreds of landlords through the same situations.*

Managing the Relationship

Now that you know how to attract and keep a quality tenant, it's time to manage the relationship. This relationship will affect your bottom line and help your asset perform at its highest level. Be sure to have the tenant execute a proper rental agreement that has been reviewed by an attorney who practices in the state where your property is located. The rental agreement defines the entire course of the relationship during tenancy and move-out, outlining how and when tenants pay their rent, who can live there, and how the property can be used. It needs to be detailed and thorough, as an invalid or improper lease can prove very costly in the long run.

As a landlord, it's also important to understand your responsibilities. The law is very clear and defined on these matters. Just because you own a house and the tenant hasn't paid doesn't mean that you can shut off the utilities if they are part of the rental agreement. Many landlords have found themselves in financial trouble because they didn't understand the legalities of renting their property.

Example: *I managed a house for an owner for several years, and he fell behind on his mortgage payments, and the bank posted a notice on the door of the property. The tenants called me and informed me that they were not going to pay their rent because the owner had not been paying the bank. I explained to the tenants that they still had to pay rent, regardless of the mortgage situation.*

The second of the month rolled around, and the tenants still hadn't paid rent. I explained to the owner that we would need to issue the correct late notice, and if they didn't pay, we would file for eviction. The owner refused to listen to me and disconnected the water heater, upon which I terminated my

agreement with the landlord and immediately informed the tenants that I was no longer managing the home.

Those tenants ultimately hired an attorney when the owner would not pay to have the hot water reconnected, filing suit against the owner for treble damages. When they won, they were permitted to remain on the property for the duration of their lease and did not have to pay rent to offset their costs and attorney fees. The owner lost the house to foreclosure.

As an owner and landlord, understand your scope of responsibilities. When it comes to managing the relationship with tenants, keep it professional. Remember, there is no room for emotion. Be respectful, make repairs in a timely fashion, and avoid personal discussions. If you use outside maintenance people, explain to them how you want things handled. Let them know what they can discuss with the tenant and which conversations to avoid.

If a problem arises that you do not feel equipped to handle, call in a professional that will take the emotion out of it. As with any other investment, many factors will contribute to the overall performance of your asset. If you are unfamiliar or do not have the resources to manage it, hire someone. A competent property manager will maximize your ROI and reduce the problems you will encounter. Seasoned professionals know the laws and have the resources to handle any issues that come their way.

To ensure a smooth relationship with tenants, show appreciation. We place a "thank you" bag in every property for our residents. Upon move-in, they are welcomed with a package that includes a roll of paper towels, two water bottles, a roll of toilet paper, hand soap, a sponge, and a bottle of all-purpose cleaner. Along with these items, we also leave a note welcoming them to the property and showing our appreciation for their tenancy. While it's a simple gesture, tenants appreciate it. It sets the tone that we value them and are here to provide them with friendly service.

Throughout my career, I have met many investors who have long-term tenants. Because of the quality and duration of these relationships, they often show their appreciation by not increasing the rent, which is <u>not</u> a good practice. We have taken over management on hundreds of properties in which the tenants are paying well below market value. Ultimately, this affects your bottom line. Regardless of the good relationships with your tenants, you need to stay connected to your market.

If demand is high and prices are increasing, you don't want to lose out on thousands of dollars. If your property should rent for $1,500, but you are only charging $1,200, that's a loss of $3,600 per year — money that you will never be able to recoup. On the flip side, when there is a surplus of rentals, prices will decrease. You don't want to lose a quality tenant because they can move around the corner for a better deal.

I counsel my investors against letting their assets deteriorate. While it is smart to extend the useful life on anything that must be capitalized for tax purposes (roofs, air-conditioning units, furnaces, septic tanks, etc.), you can't allow them to deteriorate to the point that they damage other things on the property and become a nuisance for your resident. Remember, vacancies equate to a loss of revenue and increased expenditures. Overall, this will decrease your ROI.

Instead, have a plan in place to address issues long term. Take advantage of tax benefits by spending the money just before the end of the year. Be sure to have a good maintenance plan in place for mechanical items, servicing them before high usage periods to reduce costly repair bills. Lastly, don't expect tenants to maintain the property the way you would if you lived there. Remember, they are renting for a reason.

Chapter 8 in Review:

- ⊃ The laws of supply and demand drive rentals
- ⊃ Get your unity rental ready to attract the largest candidate pool
- ⊃ Price your unit appropriately so you can make money — not lose it!
- ⊃ Your marketing efforts should make a good impression
- ⊃ Screen all applicants 18 years of age or older. Your screening should include credit, civil, criminal, sex registry, employment, and rental verification
- ⊃ Don't make deals regarding security deposits
- ⊃ Use a detailed rental agreement and have it reviewed by an attorney in your area
- ⊃ Keep the relationship professional; never get emotional
- ⊃ Understand what it means to be a landlord, and take your responsibilities seriously
- ⊃ Don't slack off; know what's going on in your marketplace, even if you have great tenants in place
- ⊃ Never let your asset deteriorate; schedule regular maintenance and budget for capital expenditure

Chapter 9.

Disasters That Could Have Been Avoided

Throughout my professional career, I've made mistakes and witnessed even more. These experiences have taught me so much. Now that I know what to avoid, I want to highlight some experiences that will help you as you begin on your path to investing.

The Importance of a Contract

Example: *My friend is a licensed real estate agent who has been in the business for many years. He had two rental properties, and when one of his friends needed a place to live, he rented one to him. The guy turned out to be a great tenant. As his landlord, my friend never increased the rent, as they hadn't established a rental agreement because the deal was* *very informal. After 10 years, the tenant contacts the landlord, announcing that he has calculated his rental payments throughout his tenancy and estimates that he has paid off the house. Now he wants to arrange for the deed to be signed over to him! The landlord informs him that he never had any intention to sell him the house and that the property was only offered as a rental.*

The problem in this scenario stems from the absence of a rental agreement. The tenant was under the impression that he was ultimately working toward purchasing the house, like a lease to purchase, but the owner was following an implied contract of tenancy. In this case, the landlord starts the eviction process, which, as I've mentioned earlier, can be lengthy and costly. The tenant disputes the fact that there was no rental agreement, saying he was under the assumption it was a lease purchase.

Finally, after several months, the tenant is removed from the property. Although technically the owner prevailed, the tenant stripped the house of everything from cabinets to drywall; there was nothing left. Devastated by this discovery, the owner went through the lengthy process of filing an insurance claim and getting the house back into shape. But the experience left him so disillusioned that he sold the property.

This situation could have been avoided if the two parties had the right conversation in the beginning. If there had been a written contract that was renewed yearly, there would have been an understanding that the deal was not a lease to purchase but a rental opportunity. In this example, the tenant and the owner were not on the same page. The relationship between tenant and landlord was not established or maintained appropriately, and, as a result, there were significant consequences.

Nickels and Dimes

As we've discussed earlier, managing the relationship with your tenants is critical. Not only will the quality of this relationship affect your bottom line, it will help your asset perform at its highest level.

> **Example:** *A tenant of one of our owners was upset because the owner wouldn't put blinds in her unit. Because the unit was rented without blinds, the owner didn't believe it was his responsibility. Despite the tenant being worried about her privacy, we agreed with the owner and denied her request. We didn't discuss the matter any further.*

When the rent was due, the tenant came into the office to pay. She presents us with $700 in loose change. Not only does she want us to count all of the coins, she also wants a receipt. Not knowing how to handle her request, I called my attorney to find out if I have to accept rent in this form. He informs me that because we accept currency, and coins are a form of currency, I have to take it. And because our policy included receipt upon payment, I also had to comply with that request.

I didn't want to stay late counting all of the coins, so I wrote her a receipt for $700. It turned out that all the money was there, but it was a valuable lesson learned. Because we refused to put blinds in her unit, she decided to exact retribution by paying her rent in coins. Even though we were acting on the behalf of the owner, looking back, I would have purchased the blinds and avoided the hassle of lugging $700 worth of coins to the bank. These kinds of situations call for you to weigh your options to determine how to prevent conflict between yourself and a tenant.

Half a House

Throughout the book, I've emphasized the importance of doing your research before purchasing a property or making a deal. The following example illustrates why it is so important to thoroughly analyze everything about the property you want to invest in so you can avoid making costly mistakes. Remember, "Buyer Beware."

> **Example:** *One of our investors purchased a property sight unseen. When we came on to manage the property, there was an existing tenant.*

Unfortunately, this investor hadn't done his homework and never checked to see if permits had been pulled on the property or if they had been closed out. In this case, this property featured an illegal addition because it hadn't been permitted, and it wasn't up to code. Since the investor hadn't done enough research, he wasn't aware of this fact.

Once the property was vacant, we started remarketing it and placed a "for rent" sign in the yard and provided the city with the required notification of intent to rent the property, as they required what amounts to a renter's license. With that notification, they charge a licensing fee and have the right to inspect the property.

In this case, the city performed the inspection and cited that the back of the house was an illegal addition, concluding that the property had to be brought up to code or the illegal addition had to be removed. The addition included a family room, a bedroom, and a bathroom. The owner initially purchased a 3-bedroom, 2-bath home that featured a family room and a living room. Without that addition, the owner was losing approximately 800 to 1000 square feet of space.

After consulting numerous contractors, it was decided that there was no way to bring the property up to code without the owner having to put approximately $75,000 into it. Because he didn't have the money to make the changes, the city refused to let him rent the property until he closed all of the permits. After much deliberation, we discovered that it would be cheaper to hire a professional to remove the back bedroom, family room, and bathroom. We then rented the property out as a 2-bedroom, 1-bath home.

Unfortunately, this removal decreased the overall value of the property, and the rent dropped from $1,100 to $800. The owner was never able to financially recover and lost the home through foreclosure. If he had only done his research, he would have discovered that the property included an illegal addition, and he would have been able to avoid the whole mess. A simple home inspection and some research could have prevented him from taking on the property originally.

When you want to find out if there are citations on a property, check your tax rolls and determine the basic square footage. You'll be able to see if any additions have been made to the property and if they are up to code.

Liability and Litigation

In some situations, we get involved after the fact. The following example illustrates a series of events that led to a lawsuit.

> **Example:** We managed a condo property in a 55+ community for an owner who had a long-term tenant in her unit. Monthly pest control services were included as part of the homeowners association fee. The tenant informed the association that they couldn't spray her unit because it is harmful to her health, and because the owner is dealing with serious personal matters at the time, she asks us to handle the situation.

The HOA didn't want to comply with this request, but we informed them that they must. (The tenant also provided a letter from her doctor confirming that the pesticide would cause harm to her health.) But the association continued to have the pest company spray outside the tenant's unit, despite our attempts to get them to stop.

The tenant filed a suit on the HOA, but the owner didn't notify us. She did call to say that she wanted us to send the tenant a nonrenewal letter. We advised against it, but the owner was set on selling the unit.

We sent the tenant a notice of nonrenewal. She was elderly and had been a good tenant, so we gave her extra time to move (90 days). After the tenant received the nonrenewal notice, she filed suit against the owner and us. We carry liability insurance, but the owner's insurance had lapsed because of life circumstances. We eventually went to court and lost. And because the owner didn't have enough money to pay the attorney fees or settlement, the court awarded the tenant the right to live rent-free in the unit for the next three years. It was also stipulated that the owner could not sell the unit until the end of the three years and that she had to pay the tenant an additional $15,000 in damages. We were ordered to pay $25,000 in damages, but our liability insurance covered all but the deductible of $5000, and the homeowners association also paid an undisclosed amount in damages.

The entire situation was very unfortunate, and, like the other situations I discussed, it could have been avoided. If the HOA had complied with the tenant's request to stop spraying pesticide around her unit, there wouldn't have been a lawsuit. Individuals who have chemical sensitivities are considered a protected class. Under federal guidelines, the HOA has no right to enforce pest control if it is harmful to the health of a resident.

Final Thoughts

For most of us, wealth doesn't happen overnight. Because the process is gradual, growing your portfolio and creating long-term wealth is a result of calculation, dedication, and a watchful eye. While investing in real estate can be challenging, if you start small and follow the guidelines I have outlined, you, too, will find prosperity. As children, we needed to learn to crawl before we could walk; investing is no different.

Take small steps to secure your financial future: surround yourself with people who have been successful in the industry, attend workshops, and research your marketplace. Avoid those "get-rich-quick" schemes that offer empty promises of "no money down." If you remain objective and view each property on its merit, you will be well on your way. Remember, never get emotional. Use straightforward strategies that will put you in the position for the best possible outcome.

I've made mistakes over the years, but they pale in comparison when I look at the success I have achieved. Without some risk, there are no rewards. It's natural to be nervous about investment decisions. Do your research, and don't get in over your head. Follow my advice, and I know that you can achieve all of your goals. Don't wait any longer; unlock the door to improve your financial future.

Conclusion

I want to thank you for spending your time reading *Obtaining Long-Term Wealth in Real Estate*. I hope that you now have the confidence and knowledge to start building your financial future. The next step on the road to your success is to put everything you have just read into practice. Using what you have learned, join your fellow investors, gain more insight into growing long-term wealth, and sign up for a free account at AllCountyProperty.com/Investors-Club.com.

The All County Investors Club is a community of like-minded real estate investors who own investments throughout the country. Its primary purpose is to combine knowledge and resources to obtain financial freedom in the rewarding real estate investment industry.

About the Author

Sandy Ferrera started her career in real estate over 30 years ago. Originally, her path was undecided, but after witnessing her parents financial struggles, she knew financial freedom was paramount. Sandy quickly realized that she had a knack for the investment side of the industry and began focusing on investing and working with fellow investors. She surrounded herself with some of the most brilliant minds in the industry — listening, learning, and practicing.

Over the years, Sandy has amassed a significant real estate portfolio, built a successful property management company, and franchised the business to expand All County® property management offices through the United States.

Thirty-five years into it, she still love the investment side of the business, and she and her husband continue to grow their real estate portfolio as well as their passion for the industry.

Glossary

Absolute auction — An auction where the sale of the property goes to the highest bidder.

Acquisition costs — The totals costs associated with purchasing a property and include not only the purchase price but also things like inspection fees, closing costs, surveys, etc.

Adjustable-rate mortgage (ARM) — A mortgage where the interest rate will periodically adjust based upon the terms and conditions and the index to which it is tied.

Americans with Disabilities Act — This civil rights law from 1990 prohibits discrimination against individuals with disabilities.

Amortization — The method used to equalize and schedule the monthly mortgage payments (including principal and interest) adjusting the proportion of principal and interest over the life of the loan.

Appreciation — The increased value of the real property over time.

Balloon mortgage — A type of mortgage that is not fully amortized over the life of the loan but will become due and payable at a preset date for the balance of the loan (which is typically a large amount). It is also known as the balloon payment.

Boot — A term commonly used in a 1031 exchange that refers to the monies received or the market value of a property.

Capitalized expenditures — The expenses used to purchase or extend the useful life of an asset and is added to the fixed basis for large expenditures that you will depreciate.

Capital gains — The increased value over the original purchase price of an investment, which is not realized until the asset is sold.

Capitalization rate (aka cap rate) — The capitalization rate identifies the potential rate of return on an investment property. *Formula = net operating income (or annual gross income minus expenses) divided by the sales price or market value of the property.*

Carrying costs — The costs associated with owning the property, which include things like mortgage payments, taxes, insurance, maintenance, etc.

Cash flow — The return after all the expenses have been deducted. Cash flow goes both ways — positive or negative. Investors always prefer a positive cash flow.

Compounded annualized ROI — This is typically stated as a percentage and represents the cumulative effect of gains or losses over time, based upon the original investment.

Contract for deed — Occurs when the seller retains the title to the property and the purchaser has a contract spelling out the agreed-upon terms to purchase the property. Once all the terms and conditions have been met, the buyer will be able to take legal title.

Conventional Loan — Any home buyer's loan that is not backed or insured by the federal government.

Credit score — A statistical number based upon a person's creditworthiness and their credit history. A credit score can range from 300 to 850. The higher the score, the more creditworthy you are. Lenders use this when evaluating loan applicants.

Depreciation — An accounting method used to calculate the decline of an asset's useful life. This is a tax advantage to many investors and is calculated based upon 27.5 years for residential property. Depreciation includes only the value of the asset, not the land.

Due diligence — Steps taken by a person to identify any potential issues and ensure no existing issues exist that would cause future financial harm.

Equity — The difference between the value of the investment versus the amount you owe you the lender. Equity represents the money you would receive if the property were sold after paying off the mortgage.

Equity line — A line of credit against your property based upon your equity.

Fair Credit Reporting Act — A law enacted to protect consumers that regulates the collection of their credit information and access to their credit reports.

Fair Housing Act — A law that was enacted to end discriminatory practices regarding the buying, selling, financing, or renting of housing in the United States.

FDIC (Federal Deposit Insurance Corporation) — an independent agency of the United States government that protects the funds depositors place in banks and savings associations; it is backed by the full faith and credit of the U.S. government.

FHA loan — A loan that is insured by the federal government in the event the buyer defaults on the loan. It covers the lender for a certain percentage of losses. This program enables many purchasers to buy with a smaller down payment.

Foreclosure — The action of the lender taking possession of a mortgaged property when the borrower has not fulfilled their obligations.

Foreclosed or bank-owned properties — Properties that the bank has taken away from the borrower because they could not fulfill the terms of the mortgage.

Homeowners or Condominium Association — Associations formed during the development of the community, which are made up of elected members of the community. Members enforce rules and regulations, resolve disputes, collect dues, and maintain the common elements.

HOA fees — Fees a property owner pays to maintain the common elements of the community.

Index rate — A benchmark index rate that reflects market conditions. As the market changes, so does the index rate. Lending institutions utilize it to determine interest rates charged for loans.

Investment — Monies or capital spent to acquire the property.

Lease purchase — Occurs when the tenant is leasing the home with an intent to purchase with part of the rent typically going toward the purchase price. This practice is often referred to as a "rent to own."

Leverage — Using other people's money to invest in real estate, most often in the form of a mortgage.

Line of credit — A loan that is taken based upon a borrower's creditworthiness and not secured by an asset, such as real property.

MIP — The insurance policy that is used for FHA loans when the purchaser is putting less than 20% down. This premium can be assessed upfront or calculated annually.

Mortgage — A debt instrument that uses the real estate as collateral and creates a lien against the property. A mortgage requires that the borrower pay back the loan and specifies all the conditions. When the loan is paid in full, the mortgage is removed.

Mortgage payment — The regular scheduled monthly payment that a borrower pays to the lender for a mortgage that is secured by real property.

National Association of Realtors® — An organization comprised of licensed real estate professionals and established to promote the real estate industry and foster professionalism within its membership.

PITI — An acronym for mortgage principal, interest, taxes, and insurance. PITI represents the total monthly payment to the lender that includes the interest on the mortgage, the principal, and the monthly escrow of taxes and insurance premiums.

PMI — An insurance policy that conventional lenders use to protect them from losses if the buyer defaults when purchasing a home with less than a 20% down payment.

VA Loan — A loan guaranteed by the United States Department of Veterans Affairs that offers eligible veterans the opportunity to purchase a home with 100% financing.

Stated income loans — A loan in which the lender does not utilize the borrower's pay stubs or income tax returns. The borrower "states" their income and is taken at their word. However, the borrowers creditworthiness and down payment are considered.

Staging — Styling and furnishing a unit to present it in a better light when offering it for sale or rent.

ROI (return on investment) — The ratio or performance measurement of the gain or loss you receive.

Sweat equity — The amount of work you put into a property to improve it via your own labor.

Wraparound mortgage — A form of secondary financing that occurs when the buyer doesn't apply for a conventional bank mortgage but, instead, signs a mortgage with the seller. The seller takes the place of the bank and accepts the new owner's monthly payments. This mortgage will be considered subordinate to any previous existing mortgages.

Wholesaling — Occurs when the investor puts a large number of properties on the market as a package and sells the entire portfolio or, most commonly, when an investor takes a property under contract to purchase and markets it to potential buyers for a higher price without ever taking title.

1031 exchange — Allows an investor to sell a property and reinvest the monies into another "like-kind" property or properties without any taxable event. These exchanges only apply to investment properties.

References and Resources

"All County Property Management Franchise." All County Property Management Franchise. Accessed July 19,2019. http://www.allcountyfranchise.com/.

"Amortization Schedule Calculator." Amortization Schedule Calculator. Accessed July 19, 2019. http://www.amortization-calc.com/.

"Featured News." HUD.gov / U.S Department of Housing and Urban Development (HUD). Accessed July 19, 2019. http://www.hud.gov/.

"FHA Loan Refinance and Home Purchase Loans at FHA.com." FHA Loan Refinance and Home Purchase Loans at FHA.com. Accessed July 19, 2019. http://www.fha.com/.

"Home." Va.gov. Accessed July 19, 2019. http://www.va.gov/.

"Information and Technical Assistance on the Americans with Disabilities Act." ada.gov Homepage. Accessed July 19, 2019. http://www.ada.gov/.

"Nar.realtor." www.nar.realtor. Accessed July 19, 2019. http://www.nar.realtor/.

CalculatorSoup, LLC. "Calculator Soup — Online Calculators." CalculatorSoup. Accessed July 19, 2019. http://www.calculatorsoup.com/.

Mymortgagestatus.com. Accessed July 19, 2019. http://www.mymortgagestatus.com/.

Return on Investment (ROI) Calculator. Accessed July 19, 2019. http://www.calculator.net/roi-calculator

"Welcome to FBI.gov." FBI. April 24, 2016. Accessed July 19, 2019. http://www.fbi.gov/.

"Your Online Resource for Tax Information & Services." IRS.com. Accessed July 19, 2019. http://www.irs.com/.

Compound Interest Calculator. Accessed on July 29, 2019 http://moneychimp.com/calculator/compound_interest_calculator.html.